Turn Your MAKE Into Money

JOHN BUEHLER

ISBN: 979-8-9855307-0-4

DEDICATION

To my wife. She is my Chief Executive, my motivation, my compass, and my love. My greatest accomplishments are all because or her.

I love you Pam.

CONTENTS

INTRODUCTION

If you spend any time at all on the internet, you know that everyone is looking for something. No matter what it is you are looking for, there are sure to be dozens, if not hundreds of people trying to convince you that their method of getting that something is the fastest, simplest route to success.

Social media is full of posts offering to show you the fastest, easiest way to become (something) in 5 days or less. Want to find love? Follow my 10 proven steps. Want more passive income? Follow these 7 proven steps. Want to start a business? You can do it in a weekend with less than $100. Trying to write a book? You can do that in 24 hours or less by doing just these 3 things!

Those last two are my favorites. Having spent most of my life running my own businesses, I have yet to find a worthwhile one that produced much more than a decent idea after a weekend. A $100 budget? Well, I have made do with very little from time to time, but as much as I'd like to encourage you, $100 probably isn't going to cut it. As for the proven steps part, there are certainly some guides, but to simplify it to a small number of steps is a bit like describing a novel in 10 words or less. You can do it, but it won't prepare you very well for the test.

Since so many people want to know the ending before the movie starts, I will do that for you right here in the introduction. Here they are, my 10 steps to creating a business from your maker projects.

1. Focus your make. Pick one item or type of item that you make, that you enjoy and can speak convincingly about, and focus on making that. Moreover, if you make a batch of 10 of the same items and they all come out differently, you may want to perfect your craft before going too much further. If your items are decidedly different for a reason, that's fine. If they just sort of come out that way, maybe you need a bit more practice first.

2. Start. Make a few of your favorite products, find a local event, get a table, and sell! Taking this first step will help you to decide if it really is what you like to do. Can you handle people's criticism? Do they respond well to your products? Did I just lose money? All sorts of things will be learned at your first in person sales event.

3. Start formalizing your business. Before you get too far into selling you will need to assess the legal structure of your business. How far is that? Well, if you will be making a profit, or selling through an avenue that requires a federal, state, or local ID other than your social security number, you are there.

4. Learn how to sell. If you have every watched the hit TV show "Shark Tank" you will see an endless train of entrepreneurs that have developed products and think that a sale price of $10 and a cost of $7 is a great deal. The cost of selling your products is likely to be bigger than the cost of their production. In many cases, those combined costs mean that you may have to walk away from the product or find a better way. If you can't learn how to sell your own product, nobody else will want to.

5. Start formalizing your make. After a few months, or maybe only weeks in business, you should start to understand how many of each product you require each month. Formalize your make processes around this. Maybe you cut parts on Monday and Tuesday, paint on Wednesday, assemble on Thursday and ship every Friday. The weekends allow you to prototype new designs. Streamlining your processes will help improve your throughput. More output per hour equals more profit.

6. Learn how to market. Marketing is different from sales. Sales happens at the end of the awareness cycle. Marketing builds that awareness. Marketing and Sales go hand in hand, but each have different tactics to help achieve the same goal. Customer acquisition.

7. Refine your business. After a short time in the market you should be able to analyze costs, sales trends and other key metrics. Tracking your data will help you to make good decisions and adjust your product mix, prices, sales channels, etc to ensure strong profits. Learning to separate business logic from emotional logic will help you to occasionally readjust your business.

8. Bring in help. There are a lot of complexities in running a business that most entrepreneurs try to take on themselves when first starting out. Legal and Accounting are two of the most common. I recommend that you have a access to a law firm very close to the beginning to help with filing your business articles. While this will cost you a bit of money, it can help you avoid costly mistakes. The same goes for accounting. While you may make it through your first year without an accountant, I recommend hiring a CPA to help you with income and taxes to make things easier.

9. Refine your make. Once you have a steady, stable set of products that flow through your business, look for ways to make your make easier. Assess whether larger or different equipment will make you more efficient. Look for ways to use common parts across numerous products. Purchase in bulk or closer to your raw materials and provide initial processing yourself. Once you start looking you will find numerous ways to make your processes easier and less costly.

10. Optimize every aspect of your business. Every product you make has a cost of goods sold (COGS). Knowing this number and actively trying to reduce it for your biggest dollar volume sellers makes your business work harder for you. Every task you add in business processes adds overhead to your costs, draining profit. Knowing where you spend time and money on these tasks allows you to minimize them.

That's it in a nutshell. These 10 steps will get you on your way. If that's what you needed to hear to get you motivated and moving, that's great! If you read through any of those ten steps and thought "that's great, but how, exactly" then this is the book for you.

1. WHAT EXACTLY IS A "MAKER"

The Merriam Webster dictionary defines a maker as "a person who experiments with creating, constructing, modifying, or repairing objects especially as a hobby". I imagine that if you are reading this book and that definition, the last bit, "especially as a hobby", made you take a bit of offense to it. Fear not, as the same dictionary offers us another definition for the word; "manufacturer" as in an automotive manufacturer.

Just as the dictionary offers multiple definitions of the word, I believe that there are multiple perceptions of who makers are and exactly what qualifies as a "make".

The maker movement that we know today is not a new thing by any stretch. In the early 1920s a couple of brothers who were interested in radio purchased some military surplus radios and decided to go into business. They would sell radios and repair parts along with tools and instruction manuals for these radios. By the late 1950s as tube radios were seeing their last hurrah and transistors were becoming popular a whole new world of electronics innovation was being unleashed. Throughout the 1960s and 70s hundreds of their RadioShack locations were frequented by makers of the day.

The 1980s and 90s saw a tidal shift from transistors to computers with build-it-yourself computers being the standard method of getting more power for decades. As the complexity of the machines that makers worked with grew, so did the variety of things that makers chose to make

21st Century Maker

The current maker environment is dominated by four types of simple machines. Vinyl and paper cutters, 3-D printers, laser cutter and engravers, and 3 axis CNC routers. The core technology used in all these machines is in fact very similar. Each are driven along one or more axis with a very simple stepper motor that keeps track of the location of the cutting or engraving device. The end effector, whether a cutter, depositor, or other tool, creates the result.

This relatively simple technology has seen hundreds if not thousands of different derivatives. Vinyl and paper cutters come in multiple size formats with it without roll feeds with some capable of cutting thin wood (though I don't recommend it). The most common small format brands, Cricut, Silhouette and Brother all provide a range of machines which include various accessory tools allowing for crimping, embossing, and engraving as well as cutting.

3-D printers can extrude a wide variety of plastic filaments including PLA (a plant-based plastic), PETG (a food grade high tensile plastic) and ABS (a high strength versatile plastic). The capabilities of these machines range from a simple single extruded creating parts smaller than 6"x6"x6" in a single color to industrial machines capable of creating parts in multiple colors and materials with virtually no limit in size. Specialty machines or attachments allow for flexible filament, filament embedded with wood or metal or even melted chocolate and other food.

Laser cutters and engravers come in a wide range of sizes, powers and laser tube type giving them the ability to cut through various material at a range of thicknesses. Today's software can carefully control the intensity of the engraver with such accuracy to allow for near photographic images to be etched into materials like wood, plastic or even stone. Some have the ability to deeply etch metals.

The addition of a 4th axis rotary component allows engraving on cylindrical objects and is a common addition to many of the mid level lasers.

CNC Routers are another area that has exploded in recent years. The ability to quickly carve shapes from wood, foam, plastic, and other non-metallic materials from the comfort of your basement or garage has an attraction like no other. The availability of heavy-duty versions of the same components used in the machines mentioned earlier has spawned dozens, if not hundreds of different 3-axis router designs.

Given the size of these machines and the intended audience (hobbies /small business), many of these machines are shipped as kits. While many view this as a bit of a roadblock, and the process can be intimidating, the process of assembling the machine itself helps the user to understand the machine at a far deeper level than the machines mentioned earlier.

I personally love CNC work as I have been in the industry for my entire life. These machines however are at a bit of a different level than vinyl cutters, 3D printers or even desktop lasers. By their nature, CNC machines chew through tough materials. They fling that material around with great force in an area that is generally open to the environment (meaning YOU) and if you happen to get in the way of these machines while they are doing their job, they will bite you. Literally.

I mention this here, not to scare you in any way, but to remind you that Making can be serious business. Heat presses burn. Lasers should be operated with correctly selected glasses for each machine. The hot end of a 3D printer is, first and foremost, HOT. The spindle of a CNC router is moving crazy fast and the tools you will use are wicked sharp. In all these environments, please use the appropriate safety precautions. I want you to be making for decades to come, keep all your digits with you for the journey.

The machines we just discussed are just a small selection of the ones that I currently use. I mention these as they are popular and help to form the basis of many small businesses today. I will introduce many more tools, processes and platforms throughout the book and my hope is that you will examine them all as you read. It is easy to focus on your current tools, such as "I use a Cricut Maker for Apparel" and miss out on opportunities like "My Apparel customers would love 3D figures or wood products of my designs".

2. IS A BAKER A MAKER?

When you say the word "Maker" I think a lot of people immediately turn to the creating physical products. Some type of a durable good that is the result of a series of steps performed on some rudimentary feed stock that gives you a tangible object that you can hold in your hands at the end. I personally believe that the concept of maker extends well beyond that.

All the machines that I discussed at the beginning of this chapter run on some type of software that drives those machines. I've spent some portion of my life writing software to make these machines do things that they previously couldn't do. I still spend some time writing software in the machining industry. I like to think that software developers, especially those who writes software that drives maker machines, are in fact, Makers.

How about the question posed above, "Is a Baker a Maker?". I certainly believe so! Combining various ingredients with a variety of methods to produce a (potentially delicious) product. That sure sounds like a Make to me. Understanding the chemistry, how small variations in the amount of ingredients, time, temperature, and method all affect the outcome.

The business side of being a baker is certainly something that all Makers can learn from. On the plus side, all the products created by a Baker are consumables. They are created, sold, and eaten. If the product is good, it is likely that they will be purchased again creating a repeat buying cycle that will hopefully continue without end. The creation of consumable products, whether they be foodstuffs or not, is of particular interest to me when I examine a business. Durable products are great and generally carry a higher margin, but how many fluffy bunnies does one person need?

Another fabulous aspect of a Baker as a Maker is the core ingredient list. The combination of Flour, Sugar, Salt, Eggs, Oil and Milk thrust into an oven can result in a hundred different flavors and textures based upon how the ingredients themselves are treated during the creation process. Toss in some flavoring, leavening agents, yeasts and extracts and there is little that you cannot create. All of these core ingredients have a relatively low cost (as a part of the finished product) and all have a long enough shelf life that they should never go bad in the course of standard business operations.

I like to contrast this with one of the T-Shirt designers that I know. They make a wide variety of designs for their shirts, provide custom logos and designs, and have a wall full of vinyl colors that looks like a rainbow crashed into a unicorn. If there is a vinyl color made today that they do not have in stock, I cannot imagine what it it. While this allows them to deliver extremely high-quality products with near infinite variety, it significantly delayed their time to profitability as all the business proceeds for the first several months went into the purchase of additional inventory. While they considered this from the onset of the business and prepared for it, selection and inventory management need to be a consideration as you get started. We will talk much more about this in the coming chapters.

The life of a Baker-Maker however is not all rosewater and honey. Operating this type of business requires you to manage your output and sales in a very coordinated manner to avoid waste. While your key inputs may have a shelf life of many weeks or months, your end products do not. Producing 5000 donuts on Monday so that you have donuts for the next three months is an idea that does not work for this type of a business. Contrast that with other maker businesses where you are dealing in durable goods and you do have the ability to create items in larger batches and build inventory that will be usable in the future.

The best baker on earth consistently sells the last one of each item they produce during the last moment of the selling opportunity for the day. If you ever meet such a baker, please let me know as I would love to talk to them. Almost every business that produces time sensitive consumables will either produce just a couple too few to meet demand or overproduce just a couple too many to meet demand. In the first case the business suffers a loss from the unmet opportunity and then the latter the business suffers a loss from unsold product.

Most businesses except these small losses as the cost of doing business. As the businesses grow however, perhaps a bakery that has multiple locations, they try to stem these losses in a variety of ways. In the case of a bakery in particular the centralized production and distribution of finished products is a common theme. This works well in many types of production environments and generally has little impact on product quality. Other times recipes are changed, or ingredients are added to extend shelf life of these products. Many times, this results in a small decline in product quality.

Never underestimate the potential cost of a small decline in product quality. Chances are that when you started reading this chapter and you came across the word "Baker", a smell or other sensory reaction happened in your brain whether you knew it or not. Some positive memory likely got invoked and deep inside you thought "Mmm warm bread" or some such thing. However, when I mentioned the change of ingredients it likely brought all of that crashing to the ground.

A new memory, one of a favorite food lost to industrialization, popped into your mind. For me it was my favorite childhood lunch snack. A thin chocolate cake topped with frosting and rolled, then covered in chocolate. One day my snack cake was no longer wrapped in aluminum foil. Instead, it was wrapped in a plastic sleeve. Curious, I thought. Then I tasted it.

What the heck did they do to my delicious chocolate cake! Not only had the wrapper change, but the smooth delicious chocolate that melted in your mouth was replaced with a heavy chocolate colored wax coating. That tiny change, designed to improve shelf life, killed the product for me. I haven't had one since.

When someone thinks of your product or your company, which feeling do you want them to feel?

3. IS A GARDEN A MAKE?

If we look for the limits of what defines a Maker and therefore, what defines a Make, perhaps one of the most unconventional Makes would be a Garden. As an avid Maker and an occasional Gardener myself, I am on the fence with this one.

What I do know however is that most Makers could learn an awful lot about running a business from a gardener. If you've ever planted a garden, you know that the basic process looks something like this; prepare the soil, plant the seed, care for the plants, water, weed, repeat. After repeating this water, weed, repeat cycle for several months your plants will begin to bring forth fruit. Or more commonly vegetables. If your soil has been well prepared, you've selected a good spot for the garden and you have provided constant care, you get to reap the rewards of your effort. After harvest the entire cycle starts all over again.

During this entire cycle you have probably had to defend your garden from a wide variety of offenders. The neighborhood bunny rabbits, deer, moles and insects would all like to take their unfair share long before you get yours. One unforeseen storm, an unexpected infection, or an unexpectedly hot summer could ruin your chances for the year. Slight variations of the weather, water, soil conditions, and general care can make the difference between a poor crop and a bountiful harvest.

Starting a business can be quite a bit like starting a garden. There is certainly risk of failure, things go wrong all the time. There is also the potential of a bountiful harvest and many of the same factors that go into a plentiful garden go into the creation of a prosperous business.

Perhaps the most important lesson that a small business can learn from a gardener is the the art of planning. Most gardeners will spend a fair amount of time in the winter determining what, how much, and where to plant in the coming spring. The best gardeners have the scheduled activities of the garden down to a science. Went to fertilize, when to thin, when to harvest, when to replant, what to plant where, how often to rotate crops. All of this is driven by a schedule created far in advance using knowledge gained from the past.

Just like a gardener, most large businesses have product managers for their product lines. One of the key responsibilities of these people is to make sure that the right products are being delivered for sale at the right time. That means planning Halloween items in March, Thanksgiving items in April and Christmas items all year round.

Proper planning can make or break your business. When life feels like constant chaos, especially around the peak sales periods, it is almost always a result of poor planning. We will talk extensively on how to structure your time to eliminate this chaos on later chapters. For now it is enough to be aware of it as you get started. Remember that chasing short term trends may get you started, and that is perfectly fine, but it is not a sustainable long-term plan and will leave you disappointed in the end.

4. OPEN THE BOX!

I follow a lot of groups that relate to Makers on Facebook, Instagram, and other social media. There is always one thread that I have a difficult time understanding. That is the "I purchased such and such a machine and I haven't even opened the box" post. Some of these people purchased their machine just a few days ago but occasionally you'll see one where it's been years. This isn't limited to posters who have purchased a small and inexpensive item either, it is as common with posters who have spent several thousand dollars on a machine and can't bring themselves to take the first step.

Every time I see one of these posts I am reminded of an episode of "Antiques Roadshow" that I saw years ago.

In this episode of antiques roadshow an older woman comes to the event and brings with her a beautiful child sized tea set and a collection of vintage paper dolls. The antique dealer is amazed at the condition of both items that she brings and asks where they were from. The older woman explains that they were her grandmothers and that both her mother and later her were only allowed to play with on special occasions.

After several minutes of going back-and-forth the dealer explains that given their fantastic condition and beauty that they are probably worth several hundred dollars. The woman exclaims well, that's nice but now that they're finally in my possession they're going to get played with! You can sense in her tone that these were some of her favorites to play with her grandmother, but she was rarely allowed to do so. Her grandmother was so afraid of breaking them that she never really put them to use.

The moral of the story is this; you will never get to the end if you never start.

Starting anything is always the hardest part. Turning your hobby into a business is not necessarily a difficult task, but getting over the fear of starting can be. I like to look at it this way. There are three ways that you can approach any task. The first is with knowledge and confidence. This is always the best way to approach anything new. Knowledge is gained through study and the acquisition of knowledge helps to build confidence.

The second approach is with knowledge and caution. This is generally the case when a topic is new to you, but you've done a bit of research and you're ready to start beginning your first few experiments. These first experiments create more knowledge and build confidence. At some point in the cycle, you begin to feel the shift to method one occurring naturally. You begin to start new projects with knowledge and confidence. This generally starts a bit slower but usually ends up with good results.

The last approach is the one that we really want to avoid that is to approach something without knowledge and with confidence. The karmic world has a special name for this, reckless abandon.

While I hope that you will avoid reckless abandon in most of your pursuits, I want to encourage you whole heartedly to open the box. Step outside of your comfort zone as much as possible as often as possible, particularly when you are starting out. Failures will happen, but provided they are small, you will recover from them and grow. Whether it is working with a new machine, learning a new piece of software, reaching out to a new group of people, or finding a new sales channel, be courageous.

Remember Newton's First Law of Motion from your days in school (perhaps long ago like mine)? An object at rest tends to stay at rest while an object in motion tends to stay in motion.

Get. In. Motion.

5. WHAT SHOULD I MAKE?

One of the most startling questions that I get from people who want to start a business is this one. What should I make? My first instinct is to blurt out something inappropriate like "Really! WTF! You are ready to start a business but have no idea what to make?", but thankfully I don't. The benefit of age has given me an increased ability to curb my initial reactions (sometimes) and instead try to provide something useful.

The other reason I have for curbing my enthusiasm is the benefit of experience. It isn't that hard to look back and recognize that it really wasn't that long ago that I would have been the one asking this same question. I am also certain that there are still many times that the questions I ask could be met with equally harsh reactions by experts in other domains which are unfamiliar to me. The fact however remains, this question is absolutely one that needs to be answered long before heading into business.

When it comes down to it, this isn't that bad of a question. The reason that I dislike it so much probably comes partly from the question itself and partly from the answers that it receives. Let me explain.

Most of the time, the person who is asking the question has developed a set of skills as a maker and has a desire to turn that expertise into a business. By asking the "What should I make" question however they aren't reflecting on their history of successful makes, they are looking for the shortest route to success. This question is often phrased as "What are your most successful products?" or some variation of that.

Regardless of how the question is worded, it is generally met with descriptions of local best sellers, seasonal items and a laundry list of products that are generally well accepted.

What's wrong with that? Nothing. At least, nothing is wrong with that from the standpoint of doing market research to determine the types of products that sell well and the general price points for which they sell. The problem that I see repeated time and time again is that these "best sellers" become duplicated in near exact form over and over ad nauseam.

When first starting your maker business it can be acceptable to produce a series of "standard" or expected products for sale locally. While the products themselves may be familiar, there may be times when you have the benefit of sole presence at a local event and the items will sell. Without some type of differentiation however, your products are unlikely to compete on a broader stage.

A product that is available with similar quality and features from numerous sellers becomes a commodity. Price becomes the primary differentiator to a commodity product and continuing to make sales of such a product becomes a race to the bottom. If he who has the lowest price wins most, sellers continue to adjust their prices down to the point where they are no longer making any, or very little, profit.

While serving a market with high-quality, low-cost products and small profit margins can work for sellers capable of maximizing their output and minimizing costs, this is typically not where you want to start your business journey. Long term success is most likely to hinge upon your ability to create products that have a unique sense of style. Products that are best in their class. Products that provide the best value to the customer. Products that most accurately capture the feelings of the buyer. These are the products to build your business on.

Rather than searching for products that sell well, start with what you know best. What you enjoy. What you want. What, and who, you love. Think first about the buyer of the product and what they want rather than the product itself. Then when designing the product, design it with that person in mind.

This is, or should be, what people mean when they talk about "focusing on a niche". Focus on a who, not a what. Find your customer and design things that they would want. The closer that your customer is to you, the better that you really know them and the better that you can serve them.

Yes, you will design products that look like the products designed by others. Everyone wants a cute bunny for Easter. When you think about all of the cute bunnies you have seen, think about "If I were to design a bunny for ME, what would it look like?". How is your bunny different? If you make it for yourself, it might look like some of the other bunnies out there, but it shouldn't look like all of them.

If you do this with all the products that you design, make, and sell, eventually you will see a style running through them. Something that may be intangible but makes all of your designs begin to feel like a collection, something that says "you".

Over time you will probably find that you sell hundreds of different products and that you have entries in all, or most, of those categories that were the "best sellers" of the others that you spoke with early on. If your products are truly unique however you should notice that, while your product may be interchangeable with other sellers' products at some level, you have found your niche. Not a niche in the traditional sense of being the only seller in a micro category. A niche as being a successful seller with a cohesive sense of style across a broad range of products.

Makers who manage to pull this off have a few things in common. What are they you ask? Loyal repeat customers who appreciate your products as well as your overall design aesthetic. Pricing power in otherwise crowded commodity markets. The ability to build not just a business, but a brand. Profitably.

None of this will be easy. Easy is copying whatever everyone else makes. At least it seems to be easy. It may help you to survive, but you will always be chasing the next thing. As each product becomes a commodity and loses value, new ones must be found. Even with solid design and some level of uniqueness, the eyes of the world will be on you. They will be asking "What should I make?" And looking to you for the answer.

6. GET TO IT

I talk to a lot of Makers who would like to begin turning their hobby into a business. Just like opening the box though, many of these makers, while skilled at their craft, cringe at the thought of starting a business. More often than not they have been making the types of products that they intend to sell for quite a while. Most have been for themselves or gifts for family, but they may have occasionally sold them to friends. Many have even made a few custom orders for friends of friends, work colleagues or for one of their kid's numerous activities. The thought of making it "real" however, even though it is what the really want, scares them.

The human mind is a funny thing as it is full of fear and phobia. One of the most common phobias is the fear of failure. The fear of failure manifests itself in a wide variety of ways but one of the most common is in the creation of irrational objections to something that we want wholeheartedly. I see this in almost every Maker that I talk to as they start out on their business journey. The number of objections that people come up with is probably limitless, but some of the most common are these:

- I can't really start until I have enough inventory.
- I'm not good enough at what I do yet to sell these.
- I don't know how to run a business.
- I need a name and business cards.

- I'm afraid I will make a mistake.
- I don't really have a business plan yet.
- I want to get my website done first.

I don't know what your personal fears are, but I'll bet that one or two of the above might have struck a nerve. What I do know for certain is one thing; If you listen to these objections and give them any room at all in your life, you will never get your business started. One objection will turn into two. Two will turn into five and five will bring along an army of continuous objections that will hold you in place for the rest of your life. If you want to turn your Make into Money, there is only one way. Forward.

Start. There is your answer, simple and straight forward. Just start.

I know what I said earlier that planning is important and that you don't want to jump into things without knowledge or without confidence. A catch 22 in the situation is always that knowledge and confidence are created by doing. When you first start out on day one of your business you don't know if your products will sell. You don't know how much your products should sell for. You don't know if your local market will like your products or which ones. You don't know what you don't know or even what questions to ask, and that is a lot.

I don't say this to be mean or negative in anyway. Chances are good that you think that you know some of the above, but until you have proven it out you don't really have a full understanding. The best way to get a full understanding is to test. The way the test is to do.

Find an outlet. A local marketplace where you can introduce your products. Nearly every city, large or small, hosts a variety of events every year. If you look hard enough you will probably be able to find a few different opportunities to sell directly to your customers each and every month. From the local craft fair to a car show to a farmers market to a festival, almost everyone should have some opportunity within a short drive of their home that they can attend to test their market. You don't need a business name, you don't need business cards, you don't need to find an accountant, You don't need to build a ton of inventory, what do you do you need is to gather information.

Most small local shows will require very little of you in terms of business information. Some will require that you have a business license from the state, primarily to ensure that you are collecting sales tax, so make sure to ask. Most of the time you can register for these small events by simply providing your own personal information and operating under the guise of a DBA. Meaning you are Joe Johnson Doing Business As "Joe Johnson".

Notice that I didn't say put it up on Facebook marketplace or post on eBay. As you were getting started it is most important to be able to sell direct to a local audience. There are many reasons for this, but I'll give you a couple of great ones right away.

First it gives you the ability to talk directly to another person about your products. Sharing your excitement about your products helps to transfer your excitement to that other person. In doing so you stand a better chance of selling your product to that person than you do an any other method. Additionally it helps you to refine your message, to determine who you are as a company and what your products really mean to people.

Secondly it gives your potential customers the ability to provide you with direct and immediate feedback. This feedback will help you to better understand your customers and to help you make better products that fit their needs. Remember that the only reason a customer is making a purchase from you, aside from the fact that you're a wonderful person, is that they like your product. Most customers want to show you what they need to help you make a better product that they are more likely to purchase. Many times, our customers will show us improvements that we would not see ourselves. Let your customers help you.

Lastly, directly interacting with customers helps you to become a more extroverted, confident person. When running a business your belief in your self can be critical. Sometimes it may even be all that you have. Building this confidence by interacting with your customers directly will help to make you a better business person.

Congratulations! Just like that you are in business.

When you are first starting out make sure that you don't get caught up in the paralysis of all the things that you *think* you need to have to be a business. Remember that the most important things about being a business is creating and selling your products. Everything else can be built over time as we will discuss right here as we move forward.

A is for Astronaut

My parents purchased a set of encyclopedias for my sister and I when I was young. This was not a small thing to do in the 1970s as each volume was quite expensive and one came every two weeks over the course of almost a year. I was home when the salesman came to the door and brought with him a copy of the encyclopedia for the letter "A". This is where my journey of learning, making, and creating all truly began.

In the early 1970s the space race was inescapable and the number of frontiers of new technology was immense. Computer technology was at its infancy. Space travel required materials that were never before even thought of. Brave men were required to do insanely dangerous things and came off looking like the calm, cool heroes they were in doing them. Thousands of the brightest men and women from across the world rushed into not just the space agency itself but dozens of support agencies and companies building systems, technologies, and components for the space race. Many of today's geeks, nerds, and titans of industry got their start in this era.

The encyclopedia for letter "A" contained a 36-page full color spread complete with a pull out of the Apollo rocket. It didn't take me more than five seconds of looking over this book to know that whatever it had to offer I wanted more of. It was truly amazing.

I'm not sure if my mother would've made the purchase had I not been sitting there at the table with her that day begging for the salesman to leave that first book with us, but she did. In fact, my mother and father not only endured the cost of a complete set of encyclopedias but numerous series of "Time Life Books", "How Things Get Made" and other sets. I was truly blessed by having the parents that I did and I am thankful every day for the curiosity that they built into me and gave me the freedom to explore.

7. GO IT ALONE

Bill Gates. Jeff Bezos. Elon Musk. Sara Blakey. All of these founders are known for their extreme tenacity. The desire to succeed and the drive to continue pushing forward against extreme adversity. The ability to reach the desired goal with what seems like sheer will. In a phrase, single mindedness.

All these founders know that nobody will believe in your dream as much as you will. Nobody will put in as much effort as you will. Nobody has the exact same vision as the one that you have in your head, and nobody can live inside you head with you and see that vision as it evolves in real time.

When you start your business, you need to consider whether you will go it alone or if you want to bring on a partner or possibly multiple partners. Going it alone is the only way that you have, and continue to have, complete control over your business. There is no better feeling on earth than having the ability to define your direction, set objectives, and focus on your one single vision.

Certainly, you will bring on help. Most likely an accountant and a lawyer will become part of your team at an early stage, but their interactions will likely only be a few times a year. With luck, at some point you will become busy enough to hire help for the daily operations. First part time and then full time. One, then two, then perhaps many.

As your business grows you will have the ability to look out at your business and the team you have assembled and think "Wow, I built that". There is no greater feeling in the world.

It is also very lonely. Understanding yourself well is important if you are to be the sole head of a business. Having strong confidence in your decisions without being closed minded is a matter of necessity. Surrounding yourself with a sound group of advisors will also be to your benefit. This should include others who have similar background to yours as well as those with differing skills and circumstances.

Most important however is that you don't wrap yourself in a personal cloak in invincibility. Confidence and pride will be two of your most powerful tools as a solo entrepreneur. If they are however placed before logic and knowledge, it can prove fatal. The best leaders know when they need help and seek it out.

8. DON'T GO IT ALONE!

Bill Gates. Jeff Bezos. Elon Musk. Sara Blakey. When I listed these entrepreneurs in the last chapter did you happen to notice that I slipped a couple by you?

While Bill Gates will forever be known as the head of Microsoft, the company was co-founded with Paul Allen. Elon Musk? Most associate him as the founder of Tesla, but his first success came at PayPal, which was a combination of Confinity, Started by Peter Thiel and two others, and his startup X.com.

When likeminded individuals bring together different skill sets to focus on a problem, the results can often be greater than that achieved by the same number of individuals working individually. Simply put, the whole is greater than the sum of its parts.

I have been a sole proprietor, a partner, and a co-founder with multiple partners throughout my career. While I enjoy the single mindedness that going it alone can bring, the ability to have a partner or two to rely on can be helpful. When the partner brings a different set of skills to the business, yet shares the vision for the company, the results can be amazing.

While you can hire to fill most positions as your company grows, having someone there with you, attached at the hip, that has as much to gain or lose as you do, can be a powerful motivation for everyone. When you are down, they can lift you up. If you hate sales and they love sales, Perfect!

Choosing a partner, or partners can be tricky though. Finding the right combination of skills, attitude and passion in others who are as committed to the cause as you can be hard.

When your company is young it is likely that it will require all hands-on deck. That is, all of the founders will need to be involved in the day-to-day operations of the business. During the early days of a business there can be no job too big or too small for any of the founders.

As the company grows it is likely that each founder will focus on one area of the company. It will also require a single leader to step up as the Chief Executive. Not co-chiefs. Not management by quorum. One single leader. Ensuring a smooth transition as the company grows begins with an understanding of how the company structure will change right from the beginning.

I will also mention that a business partnership can be quite like a marriage. A growing business can demand a great deal of your time and attention and when working with a partner you may find yourself spending more time with your partner than anyone else. Including your spouse, friends, and children. Having a good personal relationship outside of the business is critical as poor relationships between partners will eventually doom the business.

Whether to go it alone or start with a partner or two is a tough question. In the end, there is no right answer. Choose wisely and good luck.

9. WHAT'S IN A NAME

Once you've moved past what I consider the proof-of-concept stage for your business it's time to start the process of formalizing. During the proof-of-concept stage you are still feeling things out and you can run very fast and loose. Your business doesn't need a name, you don't need a consistent product mix, you don't need to take credit cards, you don't need a website, social media, or advertising. For the first few weeks, or even months, you can just be you, a person who sells a few things.

When you have decided that you have a workable model and this "thing" truly has the potential to be a business, you need to begin taking the steps necessary to make it one. One of the is to select a name. Don't underestimate the impact that this will have on just about every aspect of your business going forward.

Your business name is going to represent you and your products. It will drive your business registration, your website and domain name, email, your social media channels, and numerous other aspects of your business life. The difference between a good name and a bad name can truly be the difference between success and failure. The difference between a good name and a great name can mean even more.

While you can change your business name at any point in the future, the cost of doing so can be high and the longer you've been in this business the more difficult it will become. I think it's well worth spending time, even a considerable amount of time, to come up with a business name that truly represents who you are, what you do, and the types of products you wish to build now and in the future.

There are several philosophies you can follow to name in your business. Your business name can do it's best to convey a message about the type of products or services that you want to represent, such as "Rapid Laser Products" or "Classic Car Parts". Both names give the reader some idea of what your business does just from the title. I will tell you straight always that I like one of these much better than the other. Can you guess which one?

If you guessed Classic Car Parts, you were right. Why you ask? It emphasizes WHAT you make over HOW you make it. It shows that your business is focused on making a specific type of product (car parts) and narrows that down a bit further with the term "classic". While "classic" itself is not well defined, a tagline such as "replacement parts for classic cars from the 50s and 60s" completes the definition and can appear on all your associated literature.

Rapid Laser Products evokes a sense of the types of things that you might be making by describing the process more than the products. If you are operating as a custom laser cutting service, this name may be very fitting. If however you make and sell products, and your main manufacturing process happens to currently be laser cutting, then you are doing two things that may be unintended. First, you are not defining the types of products you make and second, you limit your customers perception of the types of products that you make. If, for example, you add other capabilities later, such as 3-D printing or metal fabrication, potential customers would never expect it based upon your company name.

Another way to select a name is to use a word or phrase that means something to people in a specific industry. Names such as Computer

Associates, International Business Machines, Hobby Lobby, and Home Depot are all descriptive of what they relate too but lay a very broad foundation of exactly what they do. All these companies have evolved over time to provide an ever-changing mix of products and/or services.

There is also a long history of using one's surname as a company name, especially in heavy industry. Ford, Chrysler, Hudson, Daimler and dozens of others dominated the automotive industry. Wang, Hewlett-Packard, Dell and others in Computers and Electronics and of course McDonalds in fast food. Most of these utilize the surname as the lead part of the name. "Ford Motor Company", "Dell Computers" and many others becomes known simply by the surname over time.

Two others conventional naming methods appear at the far ends of the naming spectrum. Names with laser focus and names with no focus at all.

Commonly found in the realm of names that are highly focused are names like "Katies Cookies", "Davids Leather Goods", "Kristas Designs" and "Hometown Kitchen Crafts". These names provide the customer with a fairly good idea of what products will be offered. Many of them will use the sellers name and, while I am not always a fan of this as it does tend to say "small" before "business", it also helps to provide an almost immediate sense of trust between the buyer and the seller. Establishing trust is an important part of the sales process and if the name itself can help to establish that trust, that's an added benefit.

Names that are obscure, have no direct connection with their products, or "nonsense names", are best left to those companies who have the resources to generate brand recognition. Names like Nike, Yahoo, Xerox and Kazoo which have had tremendous success throughout their history, could have just as easily failed like the hundreds of others which have come and gone over the years.

If you have already considered a list of names for your company, you will probably know by now that one of the biggest difficulties will be finding a descriptive name that is available to register both with your state and with your internet service provider. A long domain name, no matter how good, makes for difficult email addresses. A short domain name is, if any good at all, probably already registered. Any domain with numbers in it will need to be registered twice (i.e. 10, ten). Domains with natural spelling variations (color, colour) may need multiples and if you select anything with common misspellings, be sure to register and redirect all of them to your main name.

Obviously, we only remember the names of successful businesses and many of those have names that seem to roll off the tongue easily. Some rhyme, some flow smoothly and most seems, in some almost intangible way, to be friendly. That is the power of a good name.

10. STRUCTURING YOUR BUSINESS

By examining your response to the last few chapters, we can look at setting up your business and selecting what your legal structure will be and who will be involved. The primary considerations when choosing a business structure are legal liability, complexity of management and taxes.

Taxes
Perhaps the first thing to consider when selecting your business structure, or changing it, is the matter of how you will receive income from the business. When your business is losing money, or earning very little, how you receive money from the business is not very much of a concern. Chances are that the money you receive will all be earned income from your active participation in the business.

As your business grows, and hopefully becomes more profitable, there will be more income available to you and how you receive it can be important at various stages of the business. The difference is participating vs non-participating income. That is money you earn from working for the business and money that you earn as a benefit of being a shareholder of the business.

What exactly is the difference then, money is money, right? Not exactly. As an individual, how you earn money has a direct impact on your earnings with regards to Social Security. As a sole proprietor you are simply earning income and paying your own social security on that income up to the limits of collection as defined by the IRS. As of 2022, you will pay Social Security and Medicare taxes on the first $147,000 of earned income. Income beyond that limit continues to be taxed at normal tax rates, which coincidently increase significantly after the SSI tax drops off.

If you find your personal income growing beyond the level that you have previously earned or grows beyond what a hired replacement might normally be paid, you may want to consider a different business structure than a sole proprietorship. If a "reasonable" income for someone doing your job is $50,000 and the business is providing you with $80,000 in profit, a different structure could significantly reduce your tax on $30,000 of your income. This is the most common trigger when shifting from a sole proprietorship to an LLC or single person Corporation.

Understand that changing your method of compensation will also significantly reduce your potential Social Security income when the time for your retirement comes along. While your retirement may seem immensely far into the future, consider that your retirement earnings will depend on 35 years of your earnings and Social Security tax payments. While reducing taxes is top of mind for many entrepreneurs, it is only one consideration for your business formation.

Liability
Anytime that you produce a consumer product, that product can be used in any way deemed useful by the customer. If the customer decides to use your product in some crazily improper way which causes harm to them or someone else, the injured party may come after you, the creator, for damages. Certain business structures can protect you better than others in these cases by providing clear delineation between your personal assets and your business assets.

Every time you see a product label such as a "caution, tip may be hot!" label on a soldering iron or a "keep device away from water" sign on a toaster, it is likely there to limit liability. Sometimes these labels are there as a deterrent to people of limited knowledge, other times they are there as an after the fact warning resulting from a previous lawsuit. Instructions for proper usage and warnings against improper usage go a long way in helping to defend yourself and your company, however it may not be enough.

If you are developing and selling functional products (non-decorative items) that will end up in the hands of individuals and there is any possible way that they may be mis-used, there are two important things to consider. First and foremost is to purchase a general liability policy that could cover any loses due to a lawsuit to not disable your business. The second is to consider forming an LLC or a Corporation to provide separation between the company's assets and those of the owners. This will help to limit the liability to the assets of the company and not yours or any other owners' personal assets as well.

Notice that I said "help to" limit the liability. If, for any reason, you were aware of any design flaw or potential misuse of your product that could cause injury or death, the court may well attempt to pierce the veil of your company's liability protection and sue you individually as well.

Complexity

Each legal structure available to you will require a different level of management that, depending upon your expertise, may require you to bring in professional help. The formation of a sole proprietorship is quite simple, and the management of the business can generally be handled by the business owner. If the income is substantial, or if any of the requirements make you uncomfortable, I recommend having a CPA either prepare your taxes, or minimally, review them.

For any advanced legal structure such as an LLC or Corporation, enlisting the help of a CPA is truly a necessity. While you will need to do most of the preparation work yourself, or have someone inside the company prepare it, all final tax forms and the like should be signed off by your CPA. The company itself will file taxes for the income and expenses of the business operations while passing through your portion of the revenues as personal income. Having the same CPA file taxes for the business and the owners can streamline the process and save costs.

As you advance to a more complex legal structure for your business tax filings are not the only legal requirement that you will encounter. Some structures require a one-time filing with a simple yearly renewal. Others require "proof of ongoing operation" which entails occasional meetings of the shareholders and proper filing of the minutes of these meetings.

At a minimum, the use of an online service can ensure the proper registration of your business and filing of your paperwork. While this company can be used as your registered agent, the one who will receive legal paperwork on your behalf, I like to use a local law firm. While it may be more expensive, if a legal issue ever does arise you already have law firm to represent you that hopefully has some idea of what you do and your history.

Basic structures

When starting your business, you have a variety of business entity types to choose from. The primary role of this business structure is to define who owns the business, who shoulders the liability of the business, how the business operates and how profits are distributed. Your choices are Sole Proprietor, Partnership, Limited Liability Company, and Corporation.

While most businesses start as either a Sole Proprietor or Partnership, many will change over time to become an LLC or a Corporation. This is generally done to provided benefits in taxation, liability, or both. The general appearance of the company, how it is viewed by the public, can also be a consideration as your company grows. Remember that while it is quite easy to change from a simple structure like a sole proprietorship to a more complex structure like a corporation it can be more complicated to change back.

Sole Proprietor

The construct of a Sole Proprietorship is quite simple, you as an individual are also the company. If your company will be using your personal name as a trade name, such as being a consultant or providing custom services, you will simply use your Social Security number as your companies EIN. You may elect to use a non-registered trade name when first starting out, something like "Ellie Smith Designs", but remember that until you have legally filed this name, you have no explicit or exclusive right to it.

As a sole proprietor, you will collect income directly and all your income (gross revenue) will be reported on a schedule C addendum to your personal federal taxes. Your expenses will be deducted on this schedule as well until you derive a net profit (or loss) which gets reported back to the main page of your 1040. As discussed in other sections, you will calculate your income and employment taxes based upon this profit. These are the basic minimum requirements of being a sole proprietor.

While the absolute minimum noted above can get you up and running and works well for many independent consultants and contract workers, as a Maker you will probably want to go a bit further. The ability to operate under a business name that is not your own name requires registration. Registration of your business name is carried out through your state. To do this you will require a state registration number (TIN). For most states that requires a federal registration number (EIN) other than your social security number.

Fortunately, this registration process is fairly simple and is often bundled by the major online legal service operators so that you get a federal EIN, state TIN and Name registration all in one. While I recommend having this done with the help of a local small business attorney so that the registered agent is a local source, I have no real issue with using Legalzoom or one of the dozens of other filing services.

While taxation and filing are quite simple, the sole proprietor also carries sole liability for any damages caused by the products of the company or the actions of the business. In the case of a lawsuit, liability may extend beyond the assets of the company and into the assets of the individual. As a sole proprietor it is recommended that you carry proper insurance for your business activities.

Partnerships

The creation of a partnership defines a new legal entity that has its own EIN, TIN and registered name. The partners involved operate under a partnership agreement which allows all the partners to operate under the umbrella of the named company, but potentially with different roles and responsibilities. Many Doctors offices, law firms and other professional collectives operate as partners which allows them to share expenses for common services yet operate with near independence otherwise.

All the individuals in the partnership must be active participants in the company. Partners share in the overall profit of the partnership based upon their percentage share in the company. These profits flow through directly and are taxed only once at the personal level. Everyone within the partnership is liable for their own actions and generally partners will protect themselves with both individual and company umbrella insurance policies.

Limited Liability Company (LLC)

An LLC is, as the name implies, an entity type specifically designed to separate an individual, or group of individuals, from the company entity itself. The primary reason for the formation of an LLC is to provide separation from the individual owners and any business liability should something unfortunate occur. Any liability is limited to the assets of the company itself, not the assets of the operating partners.

The operation of an LLC is like a partnership. It works based upon an operating agreement defining what each owner is responsible for within the business. Taxation is generally managed like a series of sole proprietorships as any business profit is distributed to the owners based upon the percentage share defined in the operating agreement.

There are of course, exceptions. Though most LLCs have only 1 or 2 participants, there is no real limit to the number or type of members who can be involved. There is a limit of 100 members, all individuals, if you wish to provide pass through taxation. Members however are not limited to just individuals.

By allowing for other LLCs, partnerships, and Corporations to be members of an LLC the structure provides a way for other businesses to invest in the startup of your business. While most LLCs are very straight forward in their formation, this type of advanced structuring requires professional management.

Corporation

The formation of a corporation has long been the benchmark of a "real company" for one single reason. A corporation is the only business structure that allows for the issuance of stock. Stock is the primary fundraising vehicle for non-participating individuals to own a portion of your company. Because of this there are more rules and regulations surrounding the operation of a corporation.

While providing clear and concise separation between the company and the individuals operating the company, the company must maintain a set of somewhat complex paperwork to remain compliant. This includes proper recording of any changes in company stock ownership, maintain a proper board of directors, and filing the notes of regular board meetings.

S-Election

When you initially form your corporation, you can take an S-Election for your company. This indicates that you will be passing through the company's income to the individual owners each year as personal income. This prevents the double taxation of the company's income.

Which is for me?

First and foremost, get started. Don't let the idea of "I have to be a business before I can do anything" get in the way of starting. Start out as a Sole Proprietor, get some traction in your business, and then decide the direction you want to take. Most likely you will find yourself creating an LLC. How many members that will have will depend on you but start with one. Just you. Your LLC can add members in the future.

While the initial setup and occasional filings of a Sole-Proprietorship or an LLC can be handled by most business owners, I will once again recommend that you have at least a second set of eyes look things over. Properly forming and maintaining a corporation however is a job best left to an expert.

C is for Chili

The image below is of one of my most valuable possessions. Well, technically it is my wife's as she received it at her Bridal shower from my mom. It is my mother's chili recipe.

This recipe card tells a much bigger story than original recipe itself. You see, my mother's chili was always one of my favorites and it still is today. It almost wasn't though.

After we were married, my wife would make this chili for me once every few months, but it just wasn't the same as moms. Every time she would make it, she could tell that I wasn't enjoying it as much as I had purported to. Even she knew something wasn't quite right.

Finally, during a visit with my parents, my wife Pam asked. "Mom, I follow your recipe, but it just isn't the same!". So, they made it together later that afternoon. As my wife set out the ingredients, my mother said, "Not *that* vinegar, I never use white vinegar, it has to be cider vinegar."

Just because you know the recipe, doesn't always mean you know how to make something. When in doubt, consult an expert!

11. PRODUCT PRICING

The single most frequently asked question that I get asked by people just starting out in their business is "How much would you price this at?". The number of variations of this question in fact is startling as is the detail that comes out during the discussion. Before we discuss the how-tos of product pricing I would like to address some of the methods I see recommended that are really how-not-tos.

X times materials
There is a commonly understood practice in the construction industry that if you were to guesstimate the price of a home addition, renovation or other contractor led project that you can take the price of materials and multiply it by three. The logic behind it goes that the cost of installation of the materials is roughly equally to the cost of the materials and the cost of contractor services and overhead is also roughly the same. While this may be a widespread perception and, in some cases, turns out to be close, the problem is, it is just not true.

Using this as a pricing model is even less relevant for small businesses, especially craft type businesses. The biggest flaw is that the cost of materials varies widely from seller to seller. As an example, seller #1 purchases materials from a retail outlet but takes advantage of every 40% off sale that she can. The material cost for her best product, a led backlit display with vinyl additions, is just a bit shy of $8. Her competitor across town has found her supplies from a wholesaler. While she will have to purchase a minimum of 50 units, her cost is $2.65.

Using a simple formula like 3x material costs gives us two near identical products priced at $24 and $8. If both sellers were to attend the same event, you can pretty much guess what would happens. Most times the customer has little or no idea how much your materials cost. More importantly, they don't care. They just want to buy something they like for a price that they perceive as reasonable.

X per square inch
I can't tell you how many versions of a price per square inch chart that I have seen over the years in the vinyl sticker market. It is also seen in many other markets represented as cost per ounce, cost per finished square foot, etc. However, there is a single fatal flaw in this method of pricing. Detail.

Per unit pricing works well for mass produced or unfinished products. Every item in the grocery store will show its price along with the cost per item or the cost per ounce. Raw materials are packaged and sold in per unit measures. Flooring at $X per square foot, Sugar at $x per pound, even many of the inputs that makers use, vinyl priced per square foot, filament priced per kilo, lumber priced per board foot.

Some services are also sold with unit pricing. Cost per square foot of installation can be found with many providers such as roofers, concrete workers, flooring installers. This can be used to simplify pricing when you have a large business with many people quoting work to keep the pricing consistent. It is also expected that the level of detail (number of peaks and valleys on a roof, or doorways in a floor installation) have some average per job and the cost per unit is based upon this average.

The problem with using this for a maker-based business is that the level of detail will vary immensely from project to project. A 4x4 vinyl window sticker with a simple outline shape can be created far more quickly than a 4x4 vinyl window sticker made up of a large amount of small text. A simple pricing model like this can absolutely kill you when you get an order for 50 complex stickers at $3 each when each one takes you nearly an hour to make.

X + Y*Z + W + R squared

If you have tried to use either of the previous pricing methods and realized that you were either losing money or pricing yourself out of the market, you may have turned to a more complex "cost plus" pricing strategy. This strategy comes in about as many flavors as there are in ice cream, but they all start out about the same.

Take you material cost (X) add in your time (Y) times some pay rate that you would like to earn (Z). Next add in the cost of your machine operating (W) and then some value for additional profit (R). The "squared" in my equation is a bit of sarcasm. The sarcasm comes from having seen too many variations on this formula. The areas that make me cringe the most are as follows:

Setting a pay rate to an unrealistic number. I understand that every maker wants to make as much money as possible. Setting your pay rate at $300 per hour when you can easily replace yourself with another skilled worker at $30 per hour is just poor form. Your customer can probably figure out the cost of your materials and labor as well. When their number doesn't align with your number, they head for the exit.

Setting an overhead rate to some astronomical number. I once tried to keep track of the number of makers that expected to charge $100 per hour or more for a machine with low operational cost (110v electricity) and an initial purchase cost under $10,000. I have since run out of fingers and stopped counting. The fixed cost of operating such a machine (electricity, tooling, maintenance) is likely less than $3 per hour and the allowed depreciation for such a piece of equipment is likely to be several years and thousands of hours. I have customers running $200K+ machines and charging less.

While this method is loosely based upon some generally accepted accounting principles, those principles are for cost calculations, not for selling price. The single most important thing to remember when pricing is that it is an agreement between two people. One trying to sell an item and one trying to buy an item. The best possible price is when both parties are happy, and neither is too happy.

So, what are some actual valid pricing models? Having seen dozens, if not hundreds of different methods of arriving at a price throughout my career, there really are only two different methods of pricing. Cost based and value based. Cost based pricing is simple to understand, take the cost of producing your product and add a reasonable profit to that to arrive at your price. Value based pricing is a little more nuanced, being based upon the value that the customer perceives that it is getting from your product.

In truth, there is only one thing that matters. How much is the customer willing to pay?

There are also two different types of customers, wholesale, and retail. Pricing and profit margins will be drastically different between these two customers as their expectations are very different. Wholesale customers expect to use their buying power to purchase your products in volume at a significant discount to retail They in turn will handle the sales, delivery, and customer service for the sale.

Wholesale customers generally have a good understanding of three very important factors. First, they understand their customers and have a pretty good idea of what they will be willing to pay for your product. They also know, from previous experience, what it will cost them to sell and support your product. Lastly, they are well versed in the cost of production of most of the products that they resell as they may also create products of their own. This generally leaves a narrow range of pricing that they will find acceptable.

A wholesaler will always consider the following options: Can I make more profit if I make these myself and if so, is it worth the hassle? Can I get a similar product from someone else for less and if so, are they better to deal with? How much total margin is available in the product and am I getting an appropriate share for the work that I am doing?

End user customers are a whole different story. Customers make purchases with emotion more so than the logic of a wholesaler. This means that a single product that you offer may seem like a bargain at $30 to some customers but overpriced at $10 to others. Individual customers also enter into a sale with what is known as "Comparison bias". That is, a pre-conceived motion of how much your product should cost based upon their previous history with other similar products.

Let's look at the application of these pricing models and customers and examine what works and what doesn't. You will notice that many times the pricing model is indicative of the type of product or its market.

Cost based wholesale pricing
Most commodity products are priced on a cost basis. That last pricing method mentioned in the "don't do this sections", the X + Y*Z + W + R squared one. Well, that is the basis for cost-based pricing. You calculate your cost of time, materials and overhead and then add either a fixed amount or a percentage to the total to determine your price

When a product is available from a wide array of providers, competing over quality tends to get lost in the equation. As a market matures it is assumed that all producers make very high-quality products and that the main competitive drivers are cost, ability to deliver, and customer service.

Commodities products will also generally have a group of producers that have optimized their production processes and are extremely efficient. This efficiency allows them to produce products for less and sell them for less while still maintaining a reasonable margin, but only at scale. If you have ever looked at a product in Hobby Lobby or Michaels and wondered "How can they sell this for that little!" This is how.

This tends to create a market where fewer, largest companies prosper as only the largest can produce products effectively. While there are some other factors that your prospective customers will consider, price becomes the main method of competition and as far as price is concerned it can be a race to the bottom.

Competing in this type of market requires some form of a competitive edge. Superior knowledge, specialty equipment or some other type of differentiator will help you to succeed. While these types of markets and this method of pricing can be extremely difficult, it is also home to some of the largest and most successful companies in the world.

Value based wholesale pricing
Wholesale pricing assumes significant volume discounts. When those discounts are not available, such as when a provider gives little or no discount in an attempt to preserve their value-based pricing, competition will generally enter the market. Competition entering the market leads to excess capacity and forces prices lower. The alternative, of course, is price fixing and collusion which are crimes ☺

Protecting value-based pricing is possible at the wholesale level, but there needs to be some barrier to entry for your competition to prevent them from entering the market. The traditional barrier in this case is legal Intellectual Property Protection. Solid IP protection allows you to maintain higher than normal margins as you can restrict competition.

Pricing your products based upon value, yet still providing significant discounts to your largest wholesale customers can help you to maintain strong margins over the long term. Excessive margins will be met with backlash and the development of alternative products. Products without IP protection, are destined to become commodities over time.

Cost based retail pricing

While many first-time business owners approach their pricing using some variation of the cost-based method, also known as cost plus, there are several problems with this approach. The cost of time, materials, and overhead which your pricing is largely based upon, will likely differ greatly when compared to your competition. Additionally, this method doesn't consider how the customer feels about your prices.

Many commodity products, or products that have a wide array of alternatives selections, will end up being priced this way as competition will drive down prices. Just like cost-based wholesale pricing, your profitability (and likely survival) depend on your efficiency. Unlike wholesale delivery however, your efficiency will encompass both your product design and development skills, but your sales skills as well.

So, when is it appropriate to price your products using a cost basis method?

When making custom creations for a client it is often appropriate to work on a cost-plus basis. When determining the price of a custom project you can calculate the cost of materials, your time and overhead, and a reasonable margin for profit. When quoting a project for a customer I highly recommend that you quote based upon a "not to exceed" price. That provides the customer with a guarantee that the price will not exceed their perceived value or ability to pay.

Nothing is worse than creating something for a client, presenting them with a bill, and getting the response "Wow, I didn't expect that it would be this much. ALWAYS provide an estimate and agree upon a not to exceed price BEFORE purchasing any specialty materials or beginning any work. If, for some reason, the material prices change dramatically between the time you quote and the time you purchase, re-confirm with the customer, and agree mutually to adjust the final price.

You will notice that I have not used all caps very much in this book. The purpose behind using all caps is to make something stand out. I cannot emphasize enough that you must get agreement before starting and at any changes.

When pricing your custom products this way there is some risk. It may be possible that you are able to produce the item in half the time you estimated. Woo Hoo, extra profit! You may also find that it takes you three times as long. Guess what? You eat it. NEVER exceed your not to exceed quote. This does however mean that you might add an extra 5-10% or so to your normal profit margin to protect yourself.

Value based retail pricing
Most retail prices follow value-based pricing. At least they do when they are first introduced. Pricing your products based upon your customers perception of its value can be the best way to maximize your return. Finding the right price can be tricky.

Most products have some amount or research and development time that have gone into them. This may include several iterations of prototypes, product re-designs and the like. All the effort that goes into producing that very first product delivered to a customer should be accounted for somewhere. That somewhere is in the profit that you receive from each item you sell.

Hopefully you have come up with a product that has a great deal more value to the customer than it costs you to produce. Recovering your up-front investment depends on it. How much of that investment you recover with each item should be based upon how many of the item you expect to sell in the initial sales cycle.

Using a cost-plus calculation and adding in some portion of your investment can give you an idea of where to start when analyzing your initial price point. Notice that I said where to start. This first price doesn't consider the customers opinion. To do this you must test.

As an example, let's say that your product can be made for $5 total. You have spent $3500 on development. You know that you can easily sell 500 of these (costing $2500) in the first 6 months and you would like to recoup your investment in this time. Selling 500 the product for $12 each will get you to zero. Nobody really likes zero.

Does $12 feel like too much for the product, does it seem like too little? Maybe we think that is should sell for at least $20 based upon what it does, how cute it is, all the intangible, yet contributing factors. This is where you test. Attempt to sell the product 3 separate times at 3 separate prices, $24, $20, and $16. Do this to three same size sample of people and see what your sales look like. If you sell roughly the same number of items at all three prices, then you know that the appeal of the product if not heavily price influenced.

If you see a small variation in sales between the $16 group and the $24 group, consider if your total profit from sales at $24 outweighs the total profit at $16. If so, you may wish to set your initial price at $24 and reduce it over time if sales decline. If you see a wide variation in sales quantity between prices, perhaps twice the sales at the lower price, the customers may very well have spoken.

In my experience, truly unique products are not met with a tremendous amount of price sensitivity. Your product interested the customer and can command a slightly higher price. That said, as we have discussed before, your product is likely to be copied and pricing will begin to decline. At some point your original will become a commodity.

Final Notes
Pricing can be one of the trickiest parts of running your business. Getting your pricing just right can help you to grow a profitable venture. Getting it wrong can slowly drain you of your resources as it does so many startups. My recommendation? Carefully track your costs and your sales. Adjust your prices where you can and (I know you don't want to hear this...) discontinue products when you can't produce than at a price that leaves room for profit.

12. SELLING

"If you build it they will come". This is amongst the biggest lies ever told in a movie. When it comes to developing great products, it is probably #1. The unfortunate truth is more like "If you build it nobody will know about it and you will die poor and lonely".

As makers it is natural to place a high degree of value on the make. The process of making, the blood sweat and tears that goes into the construction of your product. The countless hours spent on new product designs, the skilled craftsmanship that makes it all possible. These are the things that many, if not most makers value. Prepare for reality to give you a giant smack across the face then. What matters in business is sales.

Sales is where, as the proverb puts it, the rubber meets the road. Certainly, having a great product is important, good customer service is important, proper pricing is important, but without a good sales plan none of these matters. In fact, I am pretty sure that you can think of examples where a great sales plan has overcome having a crappy product, poor customer service or bad pricing. Without sales, there will be no future making, no future customer support, no more anything.

Salespeople in large corporations are often some of the most highly compensated people in the organization. This is not coincidental. A great salesperson can sometimes generate several times as much revenue for the company than an average one. Sales is one of the most "fair" places in an organization when it comes to pay as almost all sales are performance based. For first time business owners, sales is also one of the most underestimated areas of their business.

If you are a fan of the TV series "Shark Tank" you will probably be able to recall dozens, if not hundreds, of episodes where the person making a pitch is shocked to find out that the sharks don't feel there is enough money in the product to make it viable. A product that cost $5 to make and has been selling for $8 is of little or no interest to the sharks. They are looking for a selling price of $15 or higher. Most people find this shocking. Most people also underestimate how much it will cost to effectively bring your product to market and sell it.

Going back to example of a large corporation, the total cost of sale may attribute 40% or more of the purchase price of the product. More products than you expect cost more to sell than they did to produce. I mention this to help you establish a mindset that says, "I have developed a great product, I am halfway there" rather than the traditional mindset of "I have a great product, customers are going to love it, they should sell like hot cakes!"

I suspect that right about now many of you are feeling a bit taken aback and either think that I am overstating the importance of sales or feeling a bit sick to your stomach because you have designed a great product before, tried to sell it and realize that I am right. I encourage you all to take a deep breath and embrace the process that is sales with all you have. You are likely to find yourself spending more time selling as your business grows than you do making.

Let's start by breaking down the steps to selling, looking at the avenues to selling and them examining the costs of selling in each of these avenues.

Simply put, selling is the act of transferring your enthusiasm for your product to someone else.

If there is only a single line from my book that I would hope you to remember, it is that one. Selling is the act of transferring your enthusiasm for your product to someone else. How you transfer that enthusiasm will depend on the product, the customer, the venue, and a host of other factors. The one thing that stays the same? Your enthusiasm. If you, or the people selling your product, don't absolutely love your product, people will know.

Selling your product starts by finding the best possible way to highlight the best features of your product to your audience. When selling at a live event, having great looking displays that showcases a wide array of goods, but not too many, is important. Don't worry if you can't show all your items so long as those you do display are strong sellers with good margin. Low margin options or poor sellers can be retrieved and shown if a customer expresses interest in something specific.

The same holds true for online sales, whether it is a dedicated website or your page on a selling platform. Make the homepage look amazing! See how it looks on a big screen, laptop, iPad and phone. Make sure that what is seen "above the fold" at the top of your page is your best sellers with good margin and your best chance to make a sale. This is your first impression, make it good. Work on navigation between your pages and place the products that sell fastest or those that earn you the most profit in the best positions.

Engage your customers! This is the reason that I love live events. As people approach your booth you can discuss your products with them. Having a solid short pitch for each of your products is important. Think about each product you display. When someone picks one up to ask about it, what will you say? If you start by blurting out the price "Those are $6!" You have missed the mark.

This is your opportunity to start a conversation. If the customer starts the conversation with a question, follow up with an answer along with additional information like "We have those in pink and yellow as well". If you start the conversation, you can talk about what influenced the design, what they are made of, anything that conveys "this is what makes these special!". This is how you form a common ground with your customer. Always remember, people buy from people. People they know, people they trust. You may only have 10-15 seconds to establish this trust so be genuine.

The same goes for online sales. That same 10-15 second description that you would orally give to an approaching customer. Those words are the basis for your online product description. The most powerful and descriptive single sentence is what goes first. This contains the few words that are guaranteed to be seen by the customer. Everything else is likely to disappear behind a "more..." button. Those remaining words matter mind you, especially to search engines, but the first line must convey your products main message. Make it a good one!

Online sales differ a bit here than direct sales. Generally, when talking with a customer at an event you are having a conversation, a give and take. This is a great way to learn about their response to your product. To learn what they like, or don't. To hear how you could improve your product. This is amazing and you don't get any of it online. These conversations are also usually short. Don't talk your customers ear off and don't allow them to do it to you. Engage, sell, thank, move on.

Online however you want to find a way to say EVERYTHING that you might say to any number of customers about your product. Your first line in the description is key. That said, use all the space you need, or can, to fully describe your product, its benefits, why it's the best, why they should buy from you, etc. When customers search for a product, they may just find yours because of something you said at the very end, something that you remember was important to that one customer two years ago who bought one of these. Sometimes every word, or keyword, counts.

Whenever possible, have your potential customer engage with the product. Whether that means having them hold it in their hands at a live event or envision it hanging on their wall in a virtual showroom, getting them to engage builds commitment. If you can get a customer to pick up, try on, hold, and compare your products, chances are good that you will make a sale. If there is some interesting online virtual method to accomplish this, people respond just as well. Virtual try on of glasses increased sunglasses sales for one company I know of four-fold.

Once your customer has engaged, especially in person, never miss the opportunity to upsell. Once a customer has committed to purchasing one item, you know that they like you and your products in general. If you can provide them with a great deal for buying two or more, they will often take it. Giving them a discount on multiple item purchases is a good deal for you too. You have already spent time with them convincing them to purchase once. It takes less time to upsell this customer than to find another. Repeat business should always, or almost always, get a discount.

Reducing friction. Anything that slows down your customers decision process or causes them to think twice about making their purchase is friction. At a live event this might be the addition of sales tax on your item at them end. When selling on an online platform it might be that taxes and shipping are a significant portion of the overall sale and cause the customer to abandon their cart. A slow website, or one that is hard to navigate also cause friction.

For live events I slightly up-price items so that I can include local sales tax. If it ends at an even dollar, it is best as local events still have a lot of cash transactions. If not, have plenty of change on hand. When selling online I have had mixed results. Some platforms see a large amount of cart abandonment when tax and shipping are added, others have very little. You will not know until you test it.

An ideal platform should allow for free shipping on specific items, or free shipping on orders over a minimum value. If you have complete control, such as on your own website, you can combine this and alert customers accordingly such as "Ordering additional items of $4.67 will make you eligible for free shipping". Voluntarily making customers aware of things like this gives them the feeling that you are looking out for them and helps to build brand loyalty. It will also increase your sales. This can truly be a win-win.

Capture data! Every customer that you meet, whether they purchase or not, is an opportunity to capture data. Every live event that I do, I will do a drawing for a small item. Winning that item requires leaving me your name, address, email, phone, etc. Usually, we get at least a name and an email address. That all goes to the mailing list and all those people were interested enough to at least view our products. They are good candidates for a newsletter email in the future.

The same is true for online customers whether they purchase or not. It can be a simple thing to have a pop up appear to collect their information when they decide to leave your page. A simple "Sorry that you didn't find anything that you liked this time. If you liked our shop, please sign up for our mailing list to get informed of any sales or new items!". Every visit provides an opportunity to gain something.

Having covered the basics of selling in generic terms, I can hear you asking the obvious questions. "How about Etsy?" "Should I sell on EBay?" "Does Facebook Marketplace still work?" "Are there other selling platforms out there?"

I personally enjoy selling at live events the most, though they can be hit or miss, and I assign a very high value to a day of my time spent at the event. Beyond person to person selling, I have sold, and continue to sell across a wide variety of platforms. Some products, such as bulk wholesale items, may only be available from my own websites, but your broadest customer access usually comes from a 3rd party platform.

Selling platforms are a bit of a give and take. They give you access to a broad audience; they take some of your profits as fees for that and generally push you into doing business their way. Several platforms, particularly Etsy, have gamified themselves to keep you interacting with them to the point that I find them becoming a nuisance. That said, Etsy and EBay provide the most complete seller experience to get a business up and running fast.

These two have the advantages of payment processing, sales tax collection, shipping integration at a discount, and the largest audiences available on the web. All of this, you pay for. I honestly feel bad for sellers who list their products, make their first sales, and then realize that they will lose money on every sale because of the listing fees, shipping costs, platform fees advertising fees, etc. are larger than their profit.

The reality is however that these platforms, with all the fees included, are some of the most cost-effective selling platforms available. Any way that you process a credit card, you will pay roughly 3%. Shipping is consistent unless you are a HUGE shipper and mail thousands of packages a day. The platform fees are simply the cost of maintaining an operation that can attract tens of thousands of customers daily. Replacing these with your own website is possible, but the simple act of attracting customers for your products is a difficult and expensive task. Selling is neither cheap nor easy.

I find selling through Amazon or Amazon Homemade to be a very effective solution, especially when using Amazon fulfillment. The fees are competitive and Amazon logistics is the best in the business. Amazon also provides for the intake of your product in quantity which reduces overall shipping costs, and their cost of product delivery is amongst the lowest in the business. Once again, you pay for this level of service.

The biggest downside to these services is not in the fees that they charge. The biggest downside is the control that they exercise over your business. The most widespread issue is payment holding. This is when the platform, on behalf of the credit card issuer, holds a portion of your payments until a certain action occurs. When dealing directly with an online service provider like PayPal, it is not uncommon for them to hold a portion of your funds for a period. This can often be as long as 30 days, which is typically the charge-back time limit provided to their customers.

Working with a merchant account through your bank will generally reduce the amount and the timeframe of these payment holds as your history with the bank builds. Platforms such as Etsy reserve the right to manage these payment holds using additional information available to them. This includes your marking the item as shipped, the customer marking it as received and positive review receipt. In some cases, this can result in your payments being held for a shorter period. In other case this can result in a larger percentage of your payment being held.

Perhaps the biggest disappointment is when a customer purchases and receives a product, leaves positive feedback and then later, but within their card issuer window, asks the credit card issuer for a refund. While this doesn't happen very often, there are crappy people in the world, and you will run into them. The credit card issuers and the platforms will almost always side with the customer, even when they are clearly in the wrong.

While there are a hundred frustrating things that can and do happen when working with any of these platforms, they provide the fastest and easiest way to introduce new products to new customers. Once those NEW customers become YOUR customers there are more cost-effective ways to continue selling to them however most of these selling platforms are so pervasive that convincing even your best customers to purchase directly from you rather than from one of these giants can be frustrating.

While I believe that direct selling to your customers is almost always best, the ubiquity of selling platforms makes it impractical to avoid them. What you can do however is approach them for what they are, one possible path to the customer. Understand their upsides and downsides, especially their costs, and adjust your pricing, products and sales techniques according to each platform.

13. WILL THIS BUSINESS MEET YOUR GOALS?

I get asked fairly frequently whether a maker starting a small business needs a business plan? My answer is simple. Yes. Now before you freak out thinking "oh my gosh why do I have to write a business plan, that sounds awful complex to me, and I like a lot of work!" understand exactly what a business plan is. A business plan, simply defined, is a roadmap of what the business will do, how it will do it for the foreseeable future, and an estimate of inputs and results.

I know that when people think of a business plan, they probably think of a 40-page document which is a prospectus for potential investors. This shows what the business does, how much product costs, what the plans are for hiring, what your cost of employment will be, what your growth potential is etc. Five lines on the back of a napkin that explain what products you make, how much those products cost to make, how many products you expect to sell in each period, how you will sell them, and what the profit on those products will be can also be a business plan.

If at some point you decide to take in outside investment into your business to help the business grow then it will certainly make sense to create a full business plan including an executive summary, a proposal, summary financials for the past three years, full financials for the past year and projections for the next 3 to 5 years. Any investor that you are asking for money is going to want to see at least this much information so that they can make a logical decision as to whether investing in your business is viable or not. If you were investing in someone else's business, you would ask too.

Doesn't it make the just as much sense to provide yourself with at least that five-line bullet point business plan so that you can make a logical decision before investing too much yourself? Many times, we get caught up and the idea and fail to investigate whether or not pursuing the idea makes financial sense or not. A huge portion of all startup businesses fail within the first two years. Many of them fail within the first three months because they cannot financially support themselves. If the owners had even done a rudimentary analysis, they would've known that they were doomed before even starting.

I don't bring this up at this point to discourage you. I bring this up so that you can do an analysis to determine whether your proposed business is going to meet your needs or not. First and foremost, I believe you need to decide what your goals are in starting your business. I like to break this down into the following levels:

1. Part time - extra income, gig work
2. A job - Self-employment full time
3. Small business - a few part-time employees
4. A business - full time employees, continuous growth
5. A company – focused on building a brand and not just products

Most small businesses start as a part-time job for the founder, grow into a full-time job for the founder, essentially providing self-employment for that one person, and then grow from there. How much growth occurs after that largely depends on the founders ability to take on employees and the complexity of running a business. Keep in mind that there really is no wrong answer, but it does help to set your goals and understand yourself and your skills when you're starting out.

Let's look at a simple scenario that does a quick analysis for a person, we'll all her Charlene, that has created a series of designs for unique T-shirts targeted at a specific industry. Charlene currently works in this industry, so she knows the potential customers well and has a good eye for design.

She also knows when and where the industry trade shows are, has connections in the industry and has enough contacts that can help her gain exposure to her potential customer base. She reasonably believes that she can sell 2200 shirts her first year with 300 coming from individual sales and 1900 coming from 3 group sales to industry events.

The event coordinators have budgeted an average of $11 per shirt and will provide both a free pass to the conference and exhibit space for Charlene to sell her other products. So far, Charlene is feeling pretty good about her prospects and considering if this has the potential to become a full-time thing. How does she know?

Doing a quick analysis, Charlene determines that her material cost for each shirt totals $6.15. Her gross margin on the first 1900 shirts will be $4.85 per shirt for a total of $9215. Sounds fantastic right? Next, she adds in the revenue from the 300 shirts that will sell at the conference. Estimating a selling price of $18 per shirt here with a material cost of $7.50 per shirt as some of these designs are more complex and some of the blanks more expensive. This adds sales of $5400 with a gross margin of $3450. Her total potential gross profit is $12,665.

At first glance, these numbers seem great to Charlene, and she is very excited about the possibilities! Before we get too excited however we need to examine our labor costs, travel, shipping and overhead.

Charlene has been making shirts for a while now and has refined her processes to be about as efficient as she can for a one-person operation. With focus and determination, she can make the 1900 shirts in about 42 hours. Since these are large orders, they will be created with high volume techniques. In this case multi-color screen printing and conveyor drying.

The remaining 300 shirts are a variety of designs, colors, and techniques. Some will be done with screen print while others will be vinyl and a few a combination of vinyl, bleaching and live ink. The complexity of these shirts, utilization of slower methods, and variety mean that batch sizes will be small and time per shirt will be much higher. These 300 shirts alone will take another 30 hours.

Before we determine what's available for labor, we need to back out our fixed costs for the conferences themselves. While Charlene received complementary passes and booth space, she will have shipping, travel, hotel, and meal expenses of roughly $2800 to attend the three shows. She could elect to skip the shows and lose the potential 300 shirt sales, but having those sales, gaining feedback from the customer as well as getting their contact information for future sales seems well worth it to Charlene.

So, what is the predicted result? If all goes according to plans, Charlene will have an after expenses margin of $9865 ($12,665 - $2800). She has 72 hours invested in the creation of the shirts. Things are looking gooooood!

But wait, we need to consider the 4 full days that were spent at the conference manning the booth. 32 hours. 3 days of design time. 24 hours. Phone calls, packaging, shipping, the general sales process. 14 hours. Another 60 hours in total. 132 hours in total were invested into making these sales. For all of her efforts, Charlene has managed to pay herself nearly $75 per hour. This is beginning to look like it could work.

Remember however, life comes with no guarantees. The shirts at the events could fail to sell potentially leaving her with $5400 less revenue and sitting on $2250 in dead inventory. This inventory number would likely be less as you wouldn't build more inventory for the second event if it failed to sell at the first. If she had invested only, say $800 in the first run of inventory, her cash position would be only $3665 ($9865 – 5400 – 800) and her "salary" on 132 hours of effort drops to roughy $27 per hour.

Certainly, she will recoup additional revenue from the eventual sale of some of that inventory she invested in as it trickles in over time. Also remember that very few small businesses stay busy 100% of the time. A lot of time and effort go into just moving the business along. If you figure that ½ the hours you work go directly into productive (revenue generating) tasks, that is a safe bet.

The good news here however is that Charlene has proven that her time, talent, and equipment can generate enough revenue to be self-supporting. If she were to hire employees to do all the production, she would be able to pay a fair wage confident that she wouldn't bankrupt herself in doing it. She has also proven that the business has the potential to generate a much higher potential wage for herself if she elects to commit to it full time and can manage to keep the sales pipeline full.

Understand as well, that we have ignored the initial investments that were made into machines and material, the ongoing cost of maintenance, operations cost, location cost and all other forms of overhead. When doing a quick analysis of this type you can ignore these until you get a ballpark figure as to whether there is really any profit in the operation or not.

Remember too that there are many ways to approach every opportunity. Had this been an individual with a far smaller initial investment, perhaps only having access to a couple of small vinyl cutters, the number of hours of effort might have made this impractical. If the designs were sent to a third party for the creation of direct transfers, the time could be less but the direct expenses would be far greater. Would the business have been viable under either of these conditions?

Researching your options for producing the types of products that you want to focus on is critical. When an item like a t-shirt can be created via a wide variety of processes (vinyl, silk screen, DTG printing, dye sublimation) you need to get out your napkin and compare options!

E is for Electricity

If you ask my father why we got a new power-line to our garage he will probably tell you that he needed more power out there to run his tools in the shop. I like to think that it was so that I had more power to run my experiments. Whatever the case, you have never seen somebody more excited to dig a 200 foot long trench from one building to another than I was!

When I first read about electricity I ran small experiments on little wire boards from RadioShack. Within a few weeks I had advanced to larger projects requiring "more power" and I was frequently blowing the fuse for the line that ran out to the garage. This is where the dance with my mother father and I began.

The dance went like this; power in the house would go out and I would run back from the garage to replace the fuse. My mother, knowing I was probably doing something that might require supervision, stopped me at the door to asks what I was doing. Gleefully I would begin my long explanation about the experiment and how exciting it was. Then we would go to the basement and replace the fuse. Like clockwork, this initiated a call to my father to ensure that what I was doing was safe for me to do before he got home. I would repeat my cheerful explanation again for my dad, hand the phone back to my mother, and await my answer.

I sometimes wonder if my father had a scorecard with him at work. One for John, one for Barb. It seemed to be a pretty even split. Sometimes I could continue, other times I would have to wait for my father to be coming home. I think he was trying to balance my mother's nervousness and my excitement. Whether he had a scorecard or not it seemed to work out quite well. My parents never broke my enthusiasm and my mother made it through without a nervous breakdown.

14. LIMITS TO GROWTH

Every business has limits to growth. These come in many forms, from reaching they maximum number of hours in a day that a machine can operate, the amount of time you personally have available, or maxing out your credit cards on inventory. Preparing for and managing these limits as you approach them is an important part of growing your business.

The smaller your business is, the more frequently you will run into these and the more dramatic their impact will seem. Don't let this worry you because every time you overcome one of these limits your business is stronger and better prepared for the next one. If you really want to operate a business, one that is larger than just yourself, there are several things that you should plan for in your first year or so.

For most makers, the first hurdle comes when they simply run out of hours in the day. Whether you have a separate job from your make business or not, there will come a time when you need to hire. Hiring someone to do part of the work that you were doing can be amazing. You have time to focus on growing your business, new product design, marketing, all the things that you need to bring in more business in the future. The downside of course comes in the short term.

Your new hire is likely to be less efficient at doing your work than you are. While they may prove to be more effective in the long term, in the short-term productivity is likely to decrease. Add to this the fact that you will have to dedicate some time to training and adding your first employee can be a real hassle. The first few months of payroll can also be a shocker if you aren't well prepared as well. All that money that was coming in for your paycheck. Well, now some of that goes to someone else first.

Making it past your first hire is a major achievement. Growing the business enough to cover their expense is a major milestone. Properly training them, letting go of some of your responsibilities, managing without micromanaging and making them productive without overburdening them can all be big steps in your personal growth. Each time it gets easier though. While your first employee may require you to double your business, your 10th only requires a small percentage increase.

The same is true when you approach other limiting factors. For most people their sense of scale, especially on a financial level, is based on the home income they have seen in their life. Purchasing a new car or truck is a major decision for most of us. Whether that car is new, or just new to us, is relative to the income level we have become accustomed to. That will carry over into your business.

Purchasing a new piece of equipment to get your maker business going requires cash flow from your personal income. Buying a vinyl cutter, 3D printer or even a small hobbyist CNC is often a big expense. As your business progresses and you look to increase your productivity you will likely be purchasing equipment that is far more expensive. The first time you acquire a $2000 machine can be nerve wracking. The first $10,000 machine even more so and the first $50,000 purchase? Yep, you may want to vomit, but you will get used to it.

Growth is an important part of your business, especially when you are first starting out. Unless you have a personal source of wealth, growth can be accomplished from cashflow or borrowing. When starting out it may be difficult to borrow, particularly in your businesses name. Borrowing with your own personal guarantee may be a valid option to keep your interest rate low, but never borrow for your business on a credit card unless you can afford to pay it in full when the bill comes.

I highly recommend building a strong relationship between your business and your bank as soon as is practical. While I never recommend borrowing to cover operational costs, borrowing for physical assets to be deployed in your business can be very beneficial. Many of the limits of growth can be overcome by keeping adequate cash flow and cash flow can be greatly improved by financing your capital goods.

15. BARRIERS TO ENTRY

I like to attend Marker Fairs, Startup Weekends, regional investor events and small business groups to see what emerging technologies are getting the most attention. At almost every event you will find clusters of individuals and small businesses that are focusing on the same, or similar problems. The largest clusters are almost always built around most economical technology because the cost of equipment involved in entering the market is low, or lower than alternative options.

Take for example 3D printing. I have been involved with 3D printing for 20 plus years. The first 3D Printer that I worked with cost more than my house, required frequent servicing and used some nasty chemicals. With the advent of Prusa and RepRap machines extruding inexpensive plastic, the industry changed seemingly overnight.

Within a few years, hundreds of companies sprung up in garages across the world. The cost of becoming a 3D Printer manufacturer dropped from the millions to the thousands. The cost of owning a machine quickly fell below a thousand dollars. Fast forward to today where a $300 machine can reliably produce parts and just about anyone can learn the technology required to operate one. The barrier to entering a whole series of businesses fell because the cost of the required technology dropped significantly.

The cost of becoming involved in a business is one of the biggest barriers to entry. While the low cost of entry level equipment may seem attractive as it allows you to take part in the business, you need to look at the impact on the marketplace. If a new low-cost piece of equipment is attracting you to a new market, you can be sure that the same equipment is attracting others into your business as well.

Staying in business often requires staying ahead of your competition. If your business is doing well and providing you with profit beyond your immediate requirements, I encourage you to evaluate what you can do to build your own barriers. Purchasing more advanced equipment may allow you to produce your products at a lower cost than others using simpler equipment. It may also allow you to improve your throughput, producing more with less.

These are the conditions that help you to build a defensive moat around your company. Our goal isn't to push our competition out of business. This is impractical and a bit mean spirited. Focus on your business and yours alone. When times are good, there is plenty of business for everyone. When times get tough however, your investment in creating these barriers to competition allow you to survive in an environment where others cannot.

While startup costs are one of the biggest barriers when entering or expanding your business, they are not the only one. Government regulations, Intellectual Property restrictions, lack of access to markets or materials and other issues can stop you in your tracks. I encourage you to look beyond these barriers for exactly that reason. When faced with a barrier or perceived barrier to entry, most people simply turn away.

Many entrepreneurs that I speak with view Government regulations as a major hurdle that they try to avoid. I view this as a tremendous opportunity as the existence of these regulations create a barrier that drives a good deal of your competition away before they even start! When your business if faced with regulation your first reaction should not be to shrink back, but to ask, "what do these requirements really mean and how can I comply with them?".

While working within the confines of a well-regulated industry can be tedious, building the expertise to work within these regulations can prove to be well worth it. Not only do these requirements often drive away potential competitors, over time the regulators themselves begin to have a vested interest in your success. Most times the rules and regulation set by government entities are designed to be in the best interest of your customers. Don't let the fear of regulation drive you away before you start!

Intellectual property issues often create a similar reaction. Rather than immediately turning away from a market due to a patent, or other legal restrictions, consider how you can work within the boundaries of the restriction. Can you obtain a license from the IP owners? Can you develop a product that is as good or better than the protected one? If so, should you seek protection for your product?

That last part is important. The same barriers that are used to keep you out of someone else's market can be used to keep others out of your market. While I have met countless makers that have received cease and desist orders from property rights holders, I have also met some who have created their own unique properties. While it is unlikely that you will create the next Mickey Mouse, your logo, character or catch phrase may well be worthy of protection. Understanding that there can be significant costs involved, if your design is truly unique, has broad appeal, and appears to have the potential to carry on for a significant time, trademark or copyright protection may well be worth considering.

16. HOLES IN YOUR BUCKET

Shipping cost, Sellers Fees, Refunds, Payment holds, carrying costs, product damage and loss, theft, and evil customers. If you consider your business as a bucket that you are actively trying to fill, all of these things are holes being poked into your bucket trying to drain off your profit as fast as you fill it.

While it may seem obvious, one of the best ways to increase your profits is to keep more of the money that you make from your product sales. All these drains above have nothing to do with the cost of goods sold, but expenses incurred after the sale. Every step you can take to minimize these costs carries throughout all your product sales.

Shipping
One of the biggest complaints that I hear from makers of all kinds is the cost of shipping products. Whether you include "free" shipping or calculated shipping, there are ways to make shipping less of an issue than it seems to be. First and foremost, you need to understand you shipping costs before you ship anything. Just like having a complete and agreed upon quotation before starting any custom work, never agree to ship a product until you are certain that you know the cost.

It doesn't matter whether you are selling the product from a storefront, at an event, or online, if you agree to ship it, you must know what the cost of shipping will be before agreeing to it. If you are selling in-person you should expect that someone, eventually, will request shipping. Whether it is for a large or bulky item, or a small item to be shipped to a friend address, be prepared. Having a small scale and tape measure will give you the ability to quickly look up just how much shipping your item to the customers zip code should cost. Don't guess. Guessing equals losing money, usually lots of it.

If you are shipping from an online store, make sure that you have an exact, tested, size and weight for each item you have listed before you list it. Being off by a half inch or a quarter ounce can shift you into a higher shipping bracket and make the difference between a profit and a loss. When you weigh and measure your item, check the pricing for slightly heavy or lighter packages. If there are significant saving for a lighter package, is there a way to safely reduce your product packaging weight?

If you are including free shipping, you need to pre-calculate shipping to three or four regions and take an average to add to your product cost. If you add free shipping on orders over a certain amount, try to craft that amount so that the customer needs to add one more item to qualify. Free shipping over $35 is likely to be less desirable for two $18 items than it would be on three $17 items. If your item prices and weights vary greatly you may unintentionally create winners and losers with a low free shipping limit.

When using a shipping aggregator like PirateShip, Shippo, or one of the seller services (Etsy direct labeling, etc) make sure to check their shipping prices against a few of your common products frequently. Their prices seem to change more frequently than USPS or UPS and nothing is more frustrating than making money on a Monday only to lose it on Tuesday.

One last thing to keep in mind when shipping: Product cost versus shipping cost. One of the most stated reasons for abandoning an online shopping cart is the total price of the product being much higher than expected. A $5 product with a $0.75 cost of shipping doesn't impact the value proposition of your item in any way. $4.85 shipping on that same product? Abandon ship!

Fees, fees, and more fees!

When you are first starting to sell online, the thought of creating a website, posting on social media, and managing online ads can feel like a daunting task. The fastest way to test the market is often to work with an existing platform like EBay, Etsy, or Facebook marketplace. All these platforms provide a variety of built-in services and all these services come at a cost.

Creating your own platform may come with high startup costs, but the ongoing costs may be a smaller than the portion of your sales extracted by someone else's. Additionally, many of these platforms require you to participate in their promotion via a contribution to their advertising pool. In almost all cases, spending this money independently will result in higher sales for your products. In a nutshell - Everything Platforms do, they do for themselves.

When starting out, these platform costs may be reasonable as the alternatives have high startup costs. As your business grows however, these fixed fee structures begin to benefit the platform more than they do the seller. As I have stated before, the cost of sales for your products is almost always higher than expect. As you establish yourself and your products prove to be strong sellers, you begin to have more leverage with respect to the cost of sales. You should plan for the eventual move to your own platform from the very start.

Refunds

Let's start with the single thing that most people can agree about with respect to refunds. Giving them stinks. That said, my rule with respect to giving refunds is that I will almost always give the customer a refund when requested. That said, I do try to set some boundaries.

Here is how I look at this. If the customer made a purchase and for some reason, any reason, decided that the product was not for them, they will not be a good advocate for my product or my company. If, however, I provide a refund, they may become a customer in the future and are more likely to be an advocate if they feel they were treated fairly. While very few satisfied customers will go out of their way to speak highly of you, almost all the unsatisfied ones will.

This is where I can almost hear you talking about all the things that are out of your control. "The customer changed their mind about the color." "The post office took 12 days to ship my parcel 40 miles." "This was a custom order; I cannot resell it!". The list goes on and on, but in the end it doesn't matter. Therefore, you must have a clearly listed set of rules on you receipts, websites, everywhere. Here are the rules that I find to be most important.

All products must be returned to qualify for a refund. All returned products must be in unused, like new condition. All product returns are subject to a 15% or $5 restocking fee, whichever is greater. Custom orders are subject to a 30% restocking fee. These simple conditions help to resolve most conflicts. The restocking fee helps to prevent too large a loss on postage. Returned products can generally be resold. Returned custom orders can be used as samples and the loss minimized with the higher restocking fee. Remember, just like finding the ideal price, neither the buyer nor the seller feels perfectly happy about the resolution, but generally both are ok.

Remember that the customer can file a dispute with the platform that you sold through and/or their credit card company. In the long run it is probably cheaper to eat the loss than to damage your relationship with your customer, sales platform or credit company.

Payment Holds

Cash flow is the lifeblood of every business. Having the money that you need when you need it to pay your bills is pretty much the number one requirement for staying in business. That said, there are dozens of things that happen in your business that try to prevent this from happening. One of the worst of these is a payment hold.

A payment hold is when your payment processor decides that for every dollar that comes in they will only pay you a percentage today and the rest in 30-60 days. Sometimes even 90 days! Every day that goes by you will have a larger and larger total accumulating in held funds until the hold is eased. Once eased, your will get more and more of your funds released until you are finally back to business as usual. Sometimes these holds are released immediately after a short period of time, other times they can drag on indefinitely. This will often depend on a profile constructed of your credit score, sales history, product type, etc. Other times this is a wholesale restriction by a processor or a platform.

To understand why your sales platform, bank or other financial service provider institutes a payment hold, you need to understand a bit about how the credit card companies work. Credit card companies expect that a certain portion of their sales will come under some sort of dispute. Whether that dispute arises from a stolen charge card, a problem with a product, a missing shipment or any of a multitude of other issues, the credit processor becomes the ultimate judge on how to handle the dispute.

As we just talked about with refunds, these credit issuers almost always side with their customer, the card holder. Many times, they know with certainty that their own customer is at fault, but simply stated, they don't care. The simplest and fastest way to settle the dispute, and keep the cardholder spending, is to side with the cardholder. They expect that you, the seller, understand this and expect some level of loss due to this process.

To hold the high ground during any potential dispute process, the credit issuer can institute a payment hold. By "high ground", I mean "hold onto your cash until they are certain that there will be no dispute". Most credit card processors will have in their contract the ability to institute a hold of whatever percentage they feel is prudent, at any time. The timing and percentage of these payment holds is likely to be at the worst possible time and it is so for a reason.

The holiday season is the busiest time for most retailers. It is also the busiest time for credit processors and the time where they see the greatest number of stolen credit cards and the greatest number of consumer driven purchase disputes. This perfect storm means that you are most likely to be put on a sudden payment hold going into the holidays. When you are busiest. This will be the time that your credit card processor, third party processor or sales platform will decide to hold up to 50% of your money for 30 days or more.

Payment holds can cause a major problem if you are not financially prepared to deal with them. Having an established line of credit allows you to finance your own receivables, essentially loaning yourself money from your line of credit to cover the gap in payments received. As those payments come in, you repay your line of credit and, excepting the interest costs, all is good.

Without access to capital, you can quickly find yourself unable to purchase the raw materials for the products that the customer has already paid for. Emergency funding can be expensive or unavailable, plan to the best of your ability to avoid this.

Loss

"It showed up broken.", "It never arrived.", "Where did that item go?". Every business will experience loss of some type during the company's history. Hopefully none of you will suffer a catastrophic loss from an unexpected event, but it does happen. Having insurance to cover loss of equipment, inventory and other physical items is a must once your business has reached a certain scale. Until that point, and even afterward, most loss comes from the tiniest of cuts.

Probably the most frequent of these tiny cuts is breakage during shipping. Finding a happy medium between the worlds lightest box and nearly indestructible packaging can be difficult. Deciding whether the cost of postal insurance is worth the received value is even more difficult. At some point in time, you will guess wrong on which package to send without insurance and sure enough, it will be the one crushed by the package handlers.

Customers also break things. They break things in every possible way. Sometimes it happens as they cut your item free from its packaging with a samurai sword. Other times they test the strength of their new acquisition by giving it the twist, tug and pull test only to find out that the glue was strong enough to hold those pieces together, but the pieces themselves can be broken by a fully grown man. Whatever the case may be, if your product fails within the first day or so of ownership, it will be coming back.

Still more items disappear into the shipping ether, never to be seen again. I think they probably end up with those items that go missing while you are busy packing up other items for a customer during the craft fair. Nobody seems to know quite what happened or how, but the result is usually the same, you are out a product.

I wish that I knew a foolproof way to make your business losses zero. The reality is that I do not. The best that you can do is to be aware of the causes of your losses, look for other potential causes, and mitigate the risks to the best of your ability without spending more to reduce those losses than the losses themselves.

Scams and other bad form

"I threw it out.", "You get zero stars!', "Oh, yes, I did dispute that charge". Sometimes, no matter how hard you try, customers will be crappy human beings. A package arrives broken, but the customer can't return it or send you pictures for insurance because they already threw it out. Your perfect transaction gets the world's worst rating because the customers' expectations changed after their package arrived. The customer has your product and has their credit card charge reversed.

Everything from poor communication to outright scams and theft is likely to have its impact on you over time. You need to stay alert as to how the most common scams work and take steps to avoid them. If working with a platform like Etsy, eBay or Shopify, keep all communications and transaction within the confines of the platform. One of the few tangible benefits that these platforms provide is for sales disputes. That said, these platforms have been shown to side with the buyer a disproportionate percentage of the time,

eBay is one of the few seller platforms that allows for bi-directional ratings. This ensures that when you run into a customer that has outright scammed you or been a terrible human in some other way, you can warn others about them. Unfortunately, eBay also makes it easy to create a new persona and leave the old one behind. Sometimes the best thing you can do is know that you yourself will not be doing business with that buyer again.

While you want to do your best to minimize loss from this wide array of issues, at some point you have to accept some small leaks and do your best with the biggest holes. I know this can be disheartening, but you cannot allow it to derail you. Focus where you can have the biggest impact, the place where you feel most rewarded. Focus on filling that bucket!

G is for gunpowder

You can't imagine how excited I was to finally get the letter G encyclopedia. You see the previous month they delivered the letter F and the F volume contains the word fireworks. The problem was, as excited as I was to understand how fireworks worked, one of the key components in fireworks was gun powder. With the arrival of the G, I now had the keys to the kingdom. Right there in black-and-white what the description of the core ingredients to gunpowder, just 3; sulfur, charcoal, and saltpeter. I had no idea what saltpeter was, but I knew that it was something with a little research I could find. Sulfur and charcoal seemed like they should be easier, we even had a bag of charcoal in the garage. With a little bit of research, and a few carefully asked questions in school, I had a plan.

My parents operated a small business in the center of town and because of that they seemed to know just about everyone. Everyone it seems included our local pharmacist where one goes to purchase saltpeter. Had I only gone to purchase a few pounds of saltpeter it may have seemed an odd but innocuous request. I however asked for sulfur and ground charcoal at the same time. I figured if I could simply acquire all three ingredients at once my life would be so much easier. As it happened the request instead garnered to call to my mother. One of many she would receive from the local businessman around town while I grew up.

I know one might think that the call to my mother would have ended this right there. But it did not. Much to the surprise of the pharmacist my mother inquired as to what those ingredients were normally used for, and he explained they were the primary ingredients in gun powder. Rather than my mother saying no she asked for me to wait at the store while she called my father.

→

An hour later I was back home with all the ingredients that I needed. After his conversation with my Father, the pharmacist even provided his insights as to what each ingredient did, how changing the percentages of each ingredient would affect the gunpowder and of course, a few safety precautions.

This might surprise a lot of people; in fact it surprises me as I look back upon it as an adult. But my father was an amazing person and rather than simply say "no you can't do that" if he felt something was dangerous, he would simply say "let's explore that together" so he could control the situation. He knew from his childhood that most of the times that young kids were simply told "no" they then went off and did it another way anyhow.

Looking back on this moment, so much of it seems surreal. In today's world a 20 man SWAT team would have been hauling my 13 year old fanny to jail while my bicycle would have been held as an article of criminal activity and sold at auction to pay for the exercise.

My father was one of my greatest mentors and taught me a lot about making so many different things. The dance that began between my mother my father and I expanded to include many of the small businesses around town and repeated itself often.

17. WHAT FIVE COLORS

When you first start your business it's important not to have every penny you have invested into inventory to get your business started. Don't get me wrong, I'm a big fan of inventory when it's used correctly. When you are starting out however keeping a narrow inventory is very much to your advantage. It helps you to have more money available to invest in other areas of your business and keeps the throughput of materials very high. While running out of stock is something to be avoided, keeping a narrow range of stock is very important when starting your business.

Whether we are talking about vinyl, wood, plastic, or metal, limiting the number of types, shapes, and colors that you keep in stock initially will help you focus. Consider this as a challenge. If you work with vinyls or plastics and were only allowed to purchase black, white and 5 other colors, what would you choose? Would you select a palette of primary colors? One of pastels? A series from a single range such as browns or blues? Perhaps you would select a range of metallics.

Working with a limited set of materials allows you to take advantage of bulk product pricing as you are purchasing larger quantities of a small set of items rather than small quantities of a larger range. This also forces you to fully examine what other products or designs you can make with the materials that you have.

Do you remember the story of George Washington Carver?

George Washington Carver was an agricultural scientist who helped American cotton farmers embrace crop rotation. While this resulted in high yields on their cotton crops, it led to an excess of peanuts and soybeans. Throughout the early 20th century Carver created nearly 300 products, both food and non-food, from these crops using every scrap of these materials.

If one very talented man can develop that many products from a peanut, surely you can find a way to design a collection of products that sticks to a common color palette. I am certain that if he had been given a laser engraver with only 4inch square scraps of acrylic to work with, he would have had at least that many ideas.

Working with a limited palette will also help you to establish a cohesive look and feel to the products that you offer. Having a shared color set lends itself well to establishing a collection of items. As your product line expands over time you can certainly bring in additional colors, materials, and options. Be mindful however that you may not wish to integrate these colors into your current offerings. Instead, you may wish to offer these new colors or materials as a new set or collection of products that reflect a theme of their own.

There is another reason to focus your color and material selection, even if you can stock limitless inventory. *Choice Overload*.

When a customer is presented with only a single choice, deciding whether they want the item is fairly simple. Will this item do something that I need or otherwise make my life better. Presenting a customer with two versions of a product requires the customer to make not one, but two choices. Do I want this? Which one do I want?

Providing a small range of diversity when selecting a product helps to drive sales by speaking to each customer's sense of self. Some people are drawn to dark colors, others to bold colors, others yet to brights or pastels. Having a small range of products also allows people who are shopping together to each select a "unique" item by choosing the same item differentiated by color, material, texture, or some other soft difference. The products themselves are the same but they haven't "copied" each other's purchase. Don't think this is a real thing? Go shopping with a pair of four-year-olds!

There is a limit however. Regardless of where or how the customer is shopping, we are always competing with others. Others with similar or even the same products provide an alternative to selecting one of your products. Many people feel that the best way to combat this is to provide the widest range of choices possible. Certainly, if I have more choice, the customer will buy from me rather than someone else, right? Not always. In fact, not usually.

Too much choice, whether in a retail shop that looks like an exploded piñata, or an online store that allows the customer to "configure" their exact product, often backfires. Many customers will be drawn to a vendor who has a very well-designed shop that expresses a singular point of view. The same goes for your products. One of the reasons that people abandon their online shopping carts is their inability to select from too broad an array of choice during checkout.

When making a purchase, people want to know that they "got it right". Chances are good that you run into this frequently yourself. How many times have you gone out for a meal and afterwards thought "I really should have gotten something different". Or heaven forbid, walked into a coffee shop with a menu of 400 items and felt disappointed with your choice afterward.

Those same feelings of excitement and disappointment can be managed in your own business. Providing customers with product choice allows them to feel more a part of the purchasing decision. It allows them to find the product that was just right for them. If presented with a limited choice, customers are generally very drawn to one item or variation over another. These customers are more likely to embrace their choice and speak positively about your products.

Customers who have been presented with numerous variations to your products? Well, some walk away unable to make a choice. Others will spend a very long time debating which variation to select. Hopefully they come to a clear and concise decision about which one they feel is "best". Or at least best for them. It is just as likely however that they never decided which variation they liked best. They simply pick one of the items they like.

Making a choice like this may however leave their mind unsettled and the customer may later regret the decision. "I really should have gotten the blue" or "Maybe the 8-inch version would have been better". The focus changes from the overall functionality or design of your product, to detailed options of the product. Too much choice has introduced a fear of missing out. This occurs even though they got an item that was closer to their "best" than it would have been with a limited selection.

If you want to provide broad choice to your customers, you can present a small selection of your best sellers and offer customization services. Kitchen cabinets are often sold this way, with a few standard choices available at a fixed price and the ability to customize from these basics. By offering your items this way you let your customers know that you are going out of your way to meet their needs while giving you the ability to charge a premium for that service. Start with a purposefully limited selection, learn your customer needs, and grow into offering broad selection.

18. WHICH HAMMER DO I USE ON THESE SCREWS?

One of the Facebook groups that I follow is a Cricut crafters group. I love this group and I love Cricut crafters as they really are my kind of people. I personally love the Cricut machine, and I enjoy creating and test new designs on one. I don't mean to single this group out, but they provide an ideal example several times a week of attempting to use the wrong tool for the job.

It's not their fault mind you, like many of the machines that are designed for maker hobbyist and small businesses, there are times when the machines are slightly oversold by their manufacturers. One perfect case in point is the ability of these small vinyl cutters to cut through wood. Can these machines cut wood? Yes and no.

I have personally tested a wide variety of small plotter cutters that say they can cut through wood and one form or another. Most of the time they show cutting through 1/8th inch or thinner Balsa wood taking multiple passes with a specialty blade. The samples generally show big swooping cuts to avoid any sharp corners or small lettering. Upon seeing this most crafters immediately think up the most intricate design that they can and set off to murdering a tree.

While I am convinced that some of these machines can cut through thin veneers and make large bold cuts through very soft, very thin wood, I am also convinced that, simply put, they shouldn't.

Wood is unlike any other material put through these machines. While materials like paper, vinyl, and even leather are heavily processed to provide uniformity and consistent material properties, wood is not. Having witnessed two pieces of wood run through the same machine one after the other with the same blade and same cutting conditions I can attest to the fact that one piece of wood may not cut all the way through after eight passes while the second piece of wood will not only be cut through, but the mat below will as well after just six.

Being familiar with alternative technologies such as laser cutters, it pains me to see the great amount of effort that is put into a wood cutting process like this only to have tragic results time and time again. I can no longer count the number of times that I have offered to Laser cut a design for someone who's efforts of ended in tears. This is why I believe it is incredibly important to understand what technologies are available and which work best for different situations.

I also understand that not every crafter or small business can afford to have one of every machine lying around, especially when some of those machines cost thousands of dollars and may only be needed occasionally for the types of projects that an individual our business creates. This leads me to the key point of this teeny tiny chapter which is this:

Of all the things you can make, the most important is friends.

A key component of one of my businesses is the design and production of blanks for use by other crafters in their businesses. I started this specifically to help meet the needs of others who could not afford alternate technologies or found it impractical to own as it isn't really "what they do". This is one of my lowest margin businesses as I believe that making friends and helping others succeed is as important to me at this point in my life as growing the bottom line.

If you find that you have a box of hammers but occasionally need a screwdriver, find someone with a lot of screwdrivers that might occasionally need a hammer. Become friends, work together, help each other out. I find that makers are some of the most open and constructive people in the universe. Most times all you need to do is ask.

19 WHERE DOES VALUE COME FROM?

Everyone knows who Mickey Mouse is. Walt Disney, and the company that he formed, have spent decades ensuring this. While the Walt Disney Company has expanded its focus far beyond the small collection of whimsical animated creatures that Walt first designed, those same few characters continue to be well tended to. The "House of Mouse" has grown into one of the most valuable properties in the world.

Mickey himself was certainly not the first character that Walt Disney ever drew, but he was one of his first characters to see widespread positive response from those that he shared him with. Mickey as he appeared in the now famous "Steamboat Willie" was the result of numerous tiny iterations of a character that was in Walt's mind for years. The Mickey we know today has seen numerous additional small changes over the decades.

Recognizing the popular response to this single character, an entire cast of characters known as the Mickey Universe were developed in just a few short years. Each of these characters helped to increase the value of Mickey. Mickeys association to these characters helped to provide them with value from their initiation.

While the creation of a unique character is truly a once in a generation event, the ability to maintain the value of a property (whether it be a brand, a design, or a product) is as important as establishing the property initially. Had Walt Disney and his fledgling company moved on from Mickey to other characters more quickly rather than continuing to tend to the characters they had created, the entire house of mouse may well have ended up just a condo.

The creation of a great product, particularly a unique one, is only the beginning of establishing its value. A logo designed as a simple swish on a piece of paper has little value. Years of associating that swish with quality products and defending said swish in any number of ways is what has given the Nike brand logo immense value.

Value starts with quality.
When you think about your products or your business, what impression do you want to leave? Most products on their own leave little or no impression. A rare product will occasionally stand out as being so good and dominant in its category that it will stand out. The products that do leave an impression are the bad ones.

If you think about your personal experiences right now, I am sure that you can think of a product that you bought recently that let you down. Are you as able to think of one that was great? While being cost conscious is important to your profitability, whatever you do, don't make crappy products. You know when you do. Just don't.

Value is built upon recognition.
A great product with no marketing plan is a product that no one will ever know about, let alone purchase. Memorable products are usually the result of long running marketing campaigns. While some products gain viral attention in one way or another, it is rare that viral attention alone will provide product recognition for more than a few months. Great products benefit from consistent, well thought out, marketing plans.

Value requires attention.

A well thought out marketing plan is a must to get your product known and selling, but that plan is not a one-time event. Maintaining your product sales requires continuous attention to your product. That might include frequent updates to the product, improvements to the product, expansion of the product line with partner products, frequent sales promotions and more.

Just like the false notion of "If you build it they will come", if you stop telling new people about it, your customer base will not grow.

Value requires defense.

From the moment you introduce your product there will be any number of others who will attempt to use your success to create their own. If your product is based upon sufficient intellectual property (having a patent, trademark, or copyright) it will require you to defend that intellectual property.

While I won't get into the merits of some of the poorer examples that I have seen, truly unique designs deserve the right to be protected by their creators. Failing to protect your IP when you are aware of infringement weakens your ability to defend it in the future. Even if you are accepting of someone's use of your design, you must take some form of action.

Granting a zero-cost license to someone using your IP in a positive way allows you to shows that you take infringement seriously without financially impacting the new licensee. If you don't protect your IP, and it becomes commonly used over a period of time, you may not be able to restrict its use when someone produced something that you don't agree with.

20 ON BEING COPIED

If you build it, they will copy it. A single cold hard truth that tends to be pervasive throughout many small sellers that I see is that, while they may have some original ideas of their own, a good deal of what they make and sell is inspired, or flat out copied, from someone else. I admit to having developed derivative products from time to time.

Sure, hundreds of graphics artists and designers make a living creating original material for craftspeople to use. Numerous free files for all types of projects exists. I use files from both purchased and free sources every day. The people who create these designs, they get copied every day as well. Some of my best designs are a combination of ideas from free files, purchased files and design tweaks that I have made to improve the design. I see these same design changes show up in other people's designs constantly.

Purely happenstance? Maybe, but the best ideas tend to float to the top and many times the changes that I (and others) may seem obvious. Occasionally I will create something that is unique and shortly thereafter I will see a similar design from another seller. Similar, but better! These are the ones that hurt the most, because someone else found a flaw in your design, or spotted an opportunity to make it better.

This is, at least at some level, part of the game. Anytime that you create something novel and show it to the world, people internalize it and make it a part of themselves. Everyone has those moments when creating something new where they think "I saw something once that might work in this situation" and they integrate it into their solution. This is a part of human nature and occurs at a subconscious level more often than people think.

Here is the difficult part. The more unique your idea is, the more effort you put into promoting it, the more time and energy you invest, the more likely it is that it will be copied. Faster. More broadly. Cheaper. Better.

This is where Intellectual Property law comes into effect.

Intellectual Property (IP) is the broad term used to represent a set of legal tools designed to protect the creations of inventors, designers, marketers, and other creatives. Patents protect invention and physical products. Copyright protects written materials and images. Trademark protects trade name related words, fonts, logos, and phrases. Each of these are generally applied in broad terms and give the owner of the legal IP the ability to protect it.

The costs related to filing to protect your creation may vary from a few hundred to thousands of dollars. That alone is generally higher than the derived value of most simple design creations, but occasionally you may come up with an idea that you feel merits the cost. When this becomes the case, it is time to make a visit to USPTO.GOV to begin your education. They have an excellent website.

An example would be the filing of a Trademark on the hashtag #GirlDad and its use on apparel. This Trademark exists and is in force today. This gives the owner the ability to claim the right to either exclusively produce apparel with this phrase or license it to others for a fee. If a creator is found using this mark they will likely be met with a cease-and-desist letter. This is fairly common, because most people would think that this meme is simply part of common culture and should be used freely.

In this particular case, that is not true as the originator of the phrase has legally claimed first use and has been granted protection. Failure to obtain approval or refrain from producing and selling goods can be met with legal action, fines, and seizure of goods. This particular trademark is an example of one that you could easily trip over without thinking about.

If you receive a cease-and-desist letter (frequently now an email) please take it seriously. If the sender can reference a legal mark (Copyright, Trademark or other) which you can verify to be valid, you must stop. Failure to do so is just plain foolish.

Want to know what else is just plain foolish? Producing good for sale that use material from anyone or anything that you have ever seen on television, in print, or at the movies. This includes any and all derivative work that you may have created yourself. Mashup of characters? Nope, don't do it. Amazing painting with black and white swoops that "sort of" (totally) reminds you of Cruella Deville? Nope, don't do it. "Snarley Graverson" grave sign that has the Harley logo shape? Sure. Hahahaha, gotcha. Nope, don't do it.

Some of the most ardent defenders of intellectual property online are those with the best brands who have the most well-known characters, imagery, and slogans. Disney, Marvel, and Warner Brothers alone represent hundreds if not thousands of characters, catchphrases, slogans, and other pieces of intellectual property.

Harley Davidson, Jeep, and every other automaker have spent decades building their brands and the use of their logos, or even visual representation of certain aspects of their vehicles, is expressly forbidden without proper licensing. The shape to the Harley Logo?

Don't even think amount using it. The Jeep seven finned grill? Nope.

Professional sports leagues from around the world (NFL NBA MLB, FIFA, etc) all look for infringement. Don't think that anyone in Oklahoma will care about your selling Manchester United shirts? Think again! College teams all restrict the use of their logos, and many are even more vigilant about pursuing infringement than the professional leagues. Most colleges extend that restriction to the college itself and all affiliates such as fraternities and sororities.

Think of it this way. That funky swish that Nike uses as a logo, how hard was that to create? Chances are it was one of dozens of quick sketches that crossed the desk in the earliest days of the company. The total development cost may have been just a few dollars. Since those early days however hundreds of millions of dollars have been spent building and promoting the brand and that simple logo. This includes a significant investment at the United Stated Patent and Trademark Office (USPTO) along with similar filings in dozens of other jurisdictions.

If you think that for a moment that Nike doesn't have a significant team dedicated to finding knockoffs, including those made by small sellers on Etsy, EBay, Facebook, or independent websites, you are very very wrong.

All this intellectual property is protected by a series of trademarks copyrights and other means which guarantees that any likeness of any of these characters etc. needs to be approved and properly licensed.

There is some leeway allowed for re-use of an item that already has a logo on it originally created by the company. Lots of licensees create items with their characters or images on for specifically for creators. The licensing fee gets paid as original item is made. Integrating these items in a safe manner into other products is generally ok. Make sure when you purchase these items that they can be included in your products and that you have a non-exclusive commercial right to use license.

If the product is modified as a part of the production process however, that will always be a different story. Fabric with logos, characters and brand names are a specific example where the fabric is licensed only for non-commercial use by the end user. In other words, no, you cannot make Disney PJs for sale from Disney fabric.

Another example might be a Budweiser crate that you are hoping to resell. That should be fine. Whitewashing around the crate to stylize it? Probably fine. Filling it with other products and selling the new kit? You just created a new product; Budweiser is the dominant visible brand, but the products included are not theirs and have no representation from them. Not going to happen.

I have seen a one of these crates repurposed by standing it on end and covering the face in plastic. This made a nicely enclosed display box. The maker then put an Edison bulb inside and was surprised to get a cease and desist? Priceless.

Modifying any logo'd product in any way that could cause harm, in this case start a fire and burn down someone's house, is a super fast way to get direct (i.e. phone call right now) interaction with a company lawyer. Please think about your products carefully and always assume that someone, heck, everyone, is watching.

21. LAUNCH-O-NOMICS

Now that we've discussed the value of originality and the sad reality of being knocked off, we can see why so many online retailers tend to focus on "product launches" for selling their new products. If you are unfamiliar with this technique, the basics of it are here:

1. Design and develop a unique product, or a product with a unique set of features.
2. Prime your existing market or followers with news of the upcoming release of your new and exciting product.
3. Finance a bulk purchase of the product for a limited release.
4. Advertise heavily over a short period of time to attract as many customers as possible to purchase your product at release.
5. As sales from advertising begin to wane, reduce the advertising spend and narrow the sales channels.
6. After the initial surge, add this product to your stable of products, but reduce advertising costs and allow sales to trickle in. Reduce price to meet competitive demand as necessary.

Many times, especially when the product has been manufactured by an offshore company for the seller, number 6 is eliminated and once stock is depleted, sales are closed. If the sales were good, a second run may be done, but understanding that a successful product launch breeds copies, that may not be the case.

Launch-o-nomics is a direct result of an environment where every item of any uniqueness is copied at lightning speed. Rather than attempting to protect the product, and then enforce the protection, the creator decides to use speed as a selling tool.

Many times, these products themselves are similar to products already on the market, but they have one or two new features that make the product more useful in some way. Once the design improvement becomes known, these other products will integrate them into their designs.

Traditionally, the creator might apply for a patent during the development process to protect their design rights. More commonly today the patent protection is filed as part of the launch process. This is done because the patent system is open system, allowing for competitors to see filings in their industry.

Regardless of any patent protection, speed to market is the key with a product launch. Being first to market allows you to dictate a higher price for your product as you are the only outlet (currently) for your unique combination of features. Understanding your market and competitors well will help you to determine how long this window of opportunity will remain open. In most cases it may only be weeks before you have your first competitor and a few months before the market is flooded with knockoffs.

This improved margin however should provide you with the ability to spend a bit more per unit of sale on this product than you might others with lower margin. This increased marketing spend allows you to reach more people faster and sell more product in a short period of time. In an ideal world, this initial marketing push could help you to capture market dominance. In the real world, things are much trickier.

Successful product launches depend on a wide array of factors. Having a great product, pricing that product exactly right, optimizing your marketing spend with lightning speed and being able to deliver in a timely manner are all keys to success. Each of these items brings with it a new set of risks.

Having a great product is key. Knowing that the product is great can be hard to do. I think it is great, you think that it is great, will the market think that it is great? Showing the product to the largest cross section of people before release helps you to gather data point on this. Showing the product to many people increases the chance that you will be copied before your release.

Getting your pricing exactly right is even more difficult. An ideal product costs nothing to produce and is worth millions to every person that sees it. Pushing the limit of price to just the right level requires having deep insight as to how many people will purchase at each price point. Pricing high gives you greater margin and profit, Yay! Pricing high makes the product less attractive to customers and more attractive to those who would copy you. Boo! Finding the sweet spot requires talent and a bit of luck.

With any marketing program, as more people purchase your product, new purchasers are hard to find. Ad platforms know this and adjust their pricing against you dynamically. In other words, if your ads are performing very well, they will reprice higher quickly. Modifying your ads frequently and running A-B tests constantly can be difficult when you are trying to accelerate as many sales as possible to an initial launch period.

When customers are purchasing a new product and paying a premium price for that product, they expect near instant delivery. This means that you will have to carry significant inventory to launch a new product. If your product is built on demand, your production capacity must be sufficient to deliver at peak output from day one. Since most product launches are inventory driven, many times they are done with borrowed money. If your sales underperform, you may get caught with excess inventory in a decreasing price model. If your sales exceed your goals, you may have missed out on some sales by the time your inventory can be refreshed.

While all these factors add complexity to introducing your product with a launch, there are many benefits to doing so as well. If you elect to introduce your products with a launch, do your research and enter into it as well informed as you can be. Launches can be an exciting and fruitful way to bring a new product to market. If you choose this route, may you have the best of luck!

H is for Helicopter

When I was about 12 years old our town had its once-a-year large item junk collection day. On that one day in late June, I think I brought home about 25 wagons full of other people's junk. To me it was a treasure trove of builders' material. One of my friends even managed to find a great gasoline engine from some large machine. I had found some long aluminum parts that looked to us like helicopter blades. Combined with other items the two of us had collected we thought for certain that we could build a helicopter. It started out quite well. We had plywood for the base, two lawnmower seats, a ton of aluminum tubing which we bent and bolted into a frame, and the engine.

The work on our helicopter continued for about two weeks as we meticulously started to put together something that sure enough began to look like a helicopter. Every evening when my father got home from work, he would check in on us and see exactly how far along we were in the process. Making sure he knew whether the motor had been running yet or how we thought we might connect from one area to the other.

The Saturday afternoon that we got the engine running again was the day that my father put a stop to the helicopter. It was the only project that I had ever started that he intervened in. It was, of course, logical for him to do so. What two 12-year-old boys had concocted in my driveway was less of a helicopter and more of a giant decapitation machine. Our initial disappointment was tempered by the fact that my father, watching our progress, reached out to a friend of his to see if he had an alternative use for the engine. As it turned out that same weekend a truck arrived with a go cart frame that fit our engine with just a bit of welding.

Sometimes a bit of redirection goes a long way.

22. WHEN DO I QUIT MY DAY JOB?

Having made the transition from corporate employee to self-employed business owner (and back) several times, I can tell you that there is nothing more exciting than quitting your job to start a new venture. If done right, this can be a smooth and easy transition. You have planned well, left your previous employer on good terms, and your business is already taking off. It can also be a terrifying, white-knuckle ride.

Let me begin by explaining that each move that I have made personally was made after significant thought and, in most cases, an immense amount of planning. My latest shift from corporate employee to self-employed was planned for and decided 105 days before I departed. One hundred and five days. This allowed me to create the best plan possible, build my pipeline and properly prepare for my new endeavor. It also allowed me to properly shift my corporate jobs activities in a way that benefitted my employer.

I will also point out that my most recent departure from corporate life was made at the end of December of 2019. My newly chosen business was heavily dependent on my ability to appear in front of people and required extensive travel. Just three months later, every income producing event that I had booked was cancelled. My planned income for the entirety of 2020, things that I had spent 105 days working on and planning for, had disappeared.

Luckily, I had planned conservatively and had sufficient funds to weather a transition to another stream of income that wasn't as dependent on the pre-pandemic world. While this may be an extreme example of bad timing, it shows that with planning and proper risk mitigation, you can succeed. I have made other transitions that would have ended badly had something similar occurred in the past. No matter what *you* plan for, the world may have other plans.

So, what considerations went into my personal planning for such a transition? Here is my list:

1. What resources do I have to rely on?
2. How long will these sustain me and my family?
3. What benefits are supplied by my current employer?
4. What is the value of these benefits to me in dollar terms?
5. Can I do without some or all of these in the short term?
6. Do I enjoy being known as an employee of this company?
7. Do I enjoy the people that I work for?
8. Do I enjoy the people that I work with?
9. Do I enjoy the people that work for me?
10. If I stay here another 5 years, will I be happy?
11. If I leave, will I have a greater impact 5 years from now?

These things basically break down into three categories, Financial, Interpersonal, Fulfillment. While only you can determine how to weigh each of these, I believe that all three of these should be part of your consideration.

For most people the primary decision will be driven by their financial situation. A recent graduate, under the age of 26, with the ability to live in their family home with parents and obtain healthcare coverage from a parent has an enormous advantage in social support when compared to a 38-year-old married with children and a mortgage. The bare necessities are easier to achieve.

For those of you young enough and with supportive parents, I cannot emphasize enough the opportunity that this presents. Your ability to take risks without a quite so staggering cost of failure looming over your head should empower you to step out into your own business venture. Understanding that many young people can't wait to get out on their own, having the option to live a financially minimalist lifestyle can provide the relief that your business needs to get started.

Conversely, a young couple with a kid or three, two new cars and a giant mortgage enters into a new venture with an extremely high minimum monthly revenue requirement. Starting a business at this stage of your life is quite common, generally driven by the need for extra funds. Safely transitioning into the business as a full-time venture often requires Herculean effort to build the business to a point where it can replace not only your full-time income, but the extra income that you have been receiving from the business.

It is not uncommon to see people in this circumstance holding down a full-time job and growing their side business to a substantial size before making the leap. Often the business will grow into an entity of its own with several full-time employees other than the owners before the owners move on full time. I have known owners who have developed business as side hustles from their full-time jobs that never move to full time payroll. I have a few friends who have grown and sold businesses at this stage without ever leaving their days jobs.

Older individuals or couples, who have gotten past the stage of raising their families, may have different financial concerns when starting a business. While not everyone in this group has lowered their cost of living compared to the previous group, those who have reached the point where their children's schooling has been paid for (finally!) May be in a better position to take a financial risk.

Having a fully employed spouse and a reasonable cost of living can create a perfect opportunity for starting a business. The experience gained from decades of mistakes can provide the confidence and the financial stability presents one of the easier opportunities to transition from a corporate job to self-employed business owner.

As you can see from these three broadly stereotypical examples, the financial concerns of each person will truly be unique. I will admit that there have been times when I have been asked "Should I quit now?" that I have almost begged the person to be patient and grow the company more before making the transition. Patience can be the hardest part but may be the most necessary when making a logical decision. Finances, and logic alone, are not the only factors when deciding when to go full time.

My youngest son loves his job. He is good at it; he is successful in the situation, and he is generally happy with it. That said, I have lost track of the number of times he has walked through the door shouting "I quit!" or "I'm done Dad!" or some such. To aid your understanding I will add that my son is highly functioning, but on the Autism spectrum. People, even people that he loves, sometimes drive him nuts.

We all have problems with other people. Sometimes it is people we work for, other times it is people we work with, or even people that work for us. It may not even be the people directly. Company policies, politics, rules, and regulations all tend to push us into working with each other in ways that we just don't like. These things tend to be like sand. Once it has been caught in between your toes long enough it is bound to rub you raw and cause pain.

When evaluating the possibility of leaving your job to devote yourself full time to your business, look at what you are leaving. Sometimes we will be leaving behind valuable personal connections. Other times we will be leaving confrontation. One case makes you want to stay, the other drives you away. If you do decide to leave, try to take with you the lessons you learned from the people you had worked with. If you had a great work environment, mimic what made it great. If not, strive to build one that others will want to work in.

Lastly, consider that impact you will have in the two different situations. Do your skills require a large organization to bring out their best? Some of mine do and that is why I have found myself going back to the corporate world to pursue opportunities. Do you think you can leave more of a mark on society if you step out on your own, or perhaps you feel that you can triple your income?

Take a cold, hard look at the future. The possible future that is, both at your current job and at the company you envision building. I like to think that everyone can envision a better future with themselves at the helm of their own business, but it isn't so for all people. You may be at an inflection point in your career with a stunning future just a few years ahead of you.

If your current side-business isn't absolutely compelling you, be patient. If it is screaming at you to get moving though, well, who am I to get in the way of that. Whatever you decide, take the time to think through the transition and make sure that the choice you make is the right one. I wish you all the best.

23 EMPLOYEES

Eventually you will reach the point where you don't have enough time in your schedule to get everything done that you want to get done. At this point you have a variety of options. You could do less, but chances are you want to do more. Hopefully you have worked on your processes and are as efficient as you can reasonably be. You could outsource, and that may be part of your solution, but outsourcing is just a variation on hiring. However you scale up, it is time to start dealing with employees.

Taking this step changes the shape of your business in a wide variety of ways. It Is the crossroad from having a side hustle, or being self-employed, to being an employer and running a "real" company. This is the point where you have to do some soul searching and decide if this is really what you want. Your decisions from here on out don't just affect you, they affect others.

There is nothing wrong with deciding that you like going it alone and you want to keep it that way. I know tons of people who are single person companies and are quite happy about it. They focus on perfecting their offerings and promoting their highest margin offerings until that is all they sell. These solopreneurs produce some of the highest per capital income in the maker business. But when they go on vacation, everything is put on pause.

In a perfect world, somewhere off in the future, when you go on vacation everything continues to hum along. The business barely misses you. This however requires you to grow your business to a sizeable operation. Each new employee puts a bit of stress on the business until that employee begins to return more than they cost. Adding employees, especially early on, can cause your profitable business to become unprofitable for a time.

If done well however, building a solid team can help you to create a resilient company that provides not only for you and your family, but for the families of your employees. Building this team won't be easy and mistakes will be made. Limiting these mistakes, and correcting them as quickly as possible, will be key to growing your business.

Your first employee
Having decided to bring on your first employee, you need to have clear answers to a long list of questions. Key among them are "Can I afford to take them on?", "What, exactly, will I have them doing?" and "How do I measure success?". There are many more questions to be answered as time goes on, but in considering your first employee, let's get past these first.

When considering "Can I afford to hire this person?" you should have the cash in your hands that is required to pay the employee for at least their trial period. How long should the trial period be? That depends on how difficult the tasks you will be asking them to do are, but I believe that you should generally know if the person can handle the job in a few weeks if they are doing basic maker tasks. The real nuts and bolts to this question come down to the numbers.

Will this person be full time or part time? What will I offer for a salary? How long of a trial period am I planning for? For your very first employee I recommend that you hire casual, 16-20 hours per week, with a 4 week trial period. Pay rate? In my area I would be offering $12-15 per hour and expecting to get a young person without a ton of experience, or someone who is looking for flexible hours. Given this I know that I need to have $1200 (80 hours at $15) in my hands to get through the first month. I also know that if this works out and the person is productive that I will be budgeting that $1200 monthly on an ongoing basis. This is, of course, the goal.

The definition of "casual" is different than "part-time" thought it is sometimes referred to as "part-time, casual". The distinction of casual is one that implies no contract or benefits but can easily become a more formalized part-time or full-time employee either after the trial period or at some point further in the future.

Casual and Part-time employees will work for you less than 32 hours per week and the schedule should have some flexibility in it so that you and the employee can agree to adjust the days and times as needed. During your trial period I recommend that you have a consistent schedule with 2-3 days each week with no less than 4 hours per day.

Now that you are spending $1200 per month for your part time employee, that part time employee needs to help you increase your revenue enough to provide at least $1200 more in profit each month so you can afford to pay them. Be prepared that this might not happen as quickly as you would like, you may find that the first month your return on this employee is $0. The second, maybe $600. The third, perhaps $1000. If you find that you are in month four and your costs still outweigh your benefits, you've probably made a mistake.

Paying your first employee can initially be done directly without withholding any taxes providing you have explained to them that they are operating as a contractor, and they will receive a 1099 at the end of the year and that you will be reporting this as income to the IRS. You will need to have them fill out a form W-9 for your records to be able to properly fill out this form. Note that I said "initially". There are rules as to what defines a contract employee and chances are that if this person passes your requirements during your trial period, they don't really qualify as a contractor.

With your new casual employee working out well and your revenues increasing in a manner that gives you confidence that this will be a longer-term solution, you will want to convert them to a real, part-time employee. Doing this is fairly simple. They fill out a W-2 form for your records, and you engage a payroll company to generate a paycheck for them on your agreed upon schedule. This can be weekly, bi-weekly, bi-monthly, or monthly per your preference. I know that employees like to get paid weekly, but I like to pay bi-weekly. Running a payroll usually has a fixed fee plus a fee per check, so reducing the number of payroll runs from 52 to 26 can be a significant savings.

Your goal should be to grow to a mix of full time and part time employees and to provide those employees with the best work environment that you reasonably can. I find that if you treat your employees well, they will treat you well. That said, you are also taking on all the risk. Bringing on your first few employees usually means that your personal income may suffer for a while. The costs of training, downtime, unproductive employees, and changes in the economy are all on you. Expecting a decent long-term return from taking this risk is not unreasonable.

Training

The first few weeks of employment are the most critical for both you and your new employee. By the time they show up for their first shift you should have a detailed plan for the entire first week at a minimum. You should know exactly what you will be training them to do and exactly what you are expecting them to produce.

During the first day you should be giving them an overview of what you do in your business. What products your make, how you make them and how you sell them. You should be carefully watching their reaction to see if there are things that they seem particularly interested in. If they have a high interest in a particular product or process and it is one where you could offload work to them it may be a win-win. Listen as much as you talk.

As you train your employees be sure to focus on a narrow set of tasks. Asking a new hire to come in to be your "assistant" and help you make 187 different products as orders come in is unlikely to be productive. Focus on just a few that they can repeat throughout the first week or so, then expand. For example, doing all of your wood cutting, or all of your printing, or all of your setup, or all of your packaging, so they get familiar with the processes involved and can be productive quickly.

People want to know that they are doing a good job and if you give them 30 random tasks the first week, they are more likely to feel like they are struggling. If you can train an employee to do one single thing at the start of their second day and they can spend the day doing that successfully, you will both be happy at the end of the day. Expands on that over the course of the next four to six weeks until you have created a path to success that will benefit you both.

If you want to see a most extreme example, look up "Sushi chef apprenticeship" where you will see that some chefs spend 2 years or more learning how to cook and fold the egg before they are allowed to touch a knife.

Hiring family
Just because your Aunt, Uncle, Niece, Nephew or crazy cousin needs a job, that doesn't mean that you should be the one to hire them. The same tends to go for your friends, neighbors, and college besties. That said, you probably have a much better feel for some of the latter than you do your own family. Particularly when you are early on in your company, consider hiring close friends or relatives very carefully. As you grow and reach a great deal of success it becomes harder and harder to not promote these people into positions of power and responsibility. If you can't picture crazy

Uncle Fred as the manager of operations, don't get it started by hiring him as a shipping clerk.

Firing

The least fun part of any business that I have ever been involved with, either as a manager or as an owner, is handling employee discipline. Whether it is calling out someone for bad behavior and trying to put together a corrective action plan, or outright firing a person, it plain old sucks. I will admit that I have generally been blessed with amazing employees and that I have had comparatively few painful incidences. If you run a business long enough though, you will eventually find yourself in a position where you will need to let someone go.

The most common time to release someone, and probably the easiest time to do so, is as they approach the end of their on-boarding process. While you do your best to ensure that the people you offer a job to are well qualified, will find the work interesting and will fit with the others in your company, it doesn't always work out that way. If you are working closely with your new hires during the training process, clearly setting goals, and continually reviewing, both you and your new employee should know if this is going to work out. If it isn't, you won't be doing anyone a favor by keeping this person on.

Once a person has been with you for a while there should be no reason, in theory, for you to dismiss them. Occasionally you will have someone whose productivity begins to slip, maybe in a radical manner, and the issue needs to be addressed. When this happens, you need to discover whether the root cause is theirs, or yours. If something has changes in your workflow and they simply have less to do, fixing their falling productivity is on you. If however they have become bored with the work, are losing interest or are otherwise unhappy you will need to address it. If, after doing your best to restructure their work and reinvigorate them, they have failed to respond, it may well be time to let them go. I have had to release people because of this a few times and each time while it feels terrible for everyone initially, both they and you are likely to be in a better place as time goes on.

While these two examples are a bit uncomfortable, everyone involved generally ends up better off when parting ways. This is not always the case. There are instances where you may need to let someone go with little or no notice. If one of your employees harasses, threatens, or otherwise acts inappropriately toward you or any of your other employees you should terminate them as soon as you are made aware and have properly investigated the situation.

This is one of those cases where having sound legal counsel that you can consult with can be important. I hope that none of you reading this will ever have to address an employee's inappropriate actions, but if you do, do so with immediacy as to allow things to linger can be far worse than any negative reaction to the dismissal.

Management

I know that you are probably just starting your business right now and thinking about hiring management for your company seems like it is a lifetime away. That may be so, but with solid execution and a little luck, you may find yourself in that position sooner than you expect. While hiring someone to take on some of the businesses management responsibilities may seem like it is just like hiring anyone else, it is, and it isn't.

When hiring someone for a management role, I try to do one thing. I try to hire people who are smarter than me. When growing your management team, finding someone with a particular set of skills that outshine yourself in some area strengthens the overall business. I have met far too many managers in far too many companies that feel threatened when they meet someone whom they feel is smarter than they are in one way or another. I understand this. They fear that if they hire someone with great talent that that person may move into the slot above them that they themselves covet. You, however, are the boss.

Smart business owners surround themselves with people who they can learn from and people they can trust. These are the two traits that I look for in a manager.

We have come a long way in this chapter. From hiring a single part-time casual employee to offload your grunt work to building a management team. New people, new equipment and new processes are the things that will transform and grow your company. Bring each of these into your company with the same degree of cautious optimism. Vet them equally, treat them all with respect and invest in them continually and your company is sure to flourish.

J is for Jet

Not every foray into making goes exactly as you hope that it does. For me my first big failure was with jet propulsion. As a 9-year-old boy, my understanding of how a jet engine works was very rudimentary and bordered on that of a rocket engine. Rocket engines were something that I understood well having built and launched dozens of Estes rockets already. One, the Vulcan 9, was a highly detailed rocket that took days to cut and assemble. The completion of this rocket coincided with my earlier completion of a butane powered engine that was going to go into a jet car. As I built this rocket however, I noticed that the fuselage was very long and had plenty of room for this jet engine. As any young boy would do, I combined two projects into one.

Three, two, one, shhhhhhhhhhhhhhh BOOOOM!

Three seconds into flight the sky exploded with the largest boom I had ever heard. My father and I stood on the edge of the football field leaning against his truck, both a bit in shock. I was on the verge of tears as the rocket that I had put so much time into was raining down in tiny pieces. My father calmly disconnected the rocket launcher from the truck battery and closed the hood.

The football field was not far from the Town hall where we could hear the emergency alarm going off. While we picked up pieces of the rocket from the football field, I'm pretty sure that our local officers were trying to figure out exactly where that large boom came from. They never did make it to the football field.

On the way home we stopped for Ice cream and my father's consolations ranged from "well, at least it wasn't painted yet" to "it really went up fast!". I think deep down inside he was just glad nobody got hurt. From that day forward rockets always had Estes engines in them even if they were a bit expensive and hard to get.

24 PRODUCT MANAGEMENT

Unless you are running your business in a Develop, Launch, Repeat cycle, your products will benefit from refinement as time goes on. Even if you are running a continuous launch type business, learning from each new product and integrating that learning into your product production processes is very important, especially to your bottom line.

Product Roadmap
Jumping from one "hot product" to the next may seem like a great way to start a business, but in doing so you are giving up control of your own product development. When you follow the crowd, you are depending on the crowd to get it right. I am not saying that you should never introduce your own version of another product. What I am saying is, wouldn't it be nice to not have to. Having an plan for what products you will develop next resolves this.

Your product roadmap is essentially a timeline of activities that you would like to take over the next several months to improve your product offerings. It should include improvements to your existing products as well as expansion of the current product line. It may include allocating time to seek out new ways to make your products more efficiently, or dedicated time to investigate new designs or new products.

When I work on a roadmap, I focus on three things. Improve, Expand, Simplify. By defining a fixed number of things that you want to achieve during a fixed amount of time, you set a (hopefully realistic) target of improvements for your products.

Competitive Analysis

Another important part of managing your products, and your company, is understanding the competitive landscape that you operate in. Remember that every product has competition. Even if you are the only person on earth who makes a specific product, you are competing for a customer's attention and dollars. A customer can select another seller's alternative product over yours for any number of reasons.

Knowing the value proposition that others offer to your customer base helps you to answer the single most important question in selling; "Why should someone buy my product from me rather than any other product from someone else?". If you can put yourself in the shoes of the customer and evaluate your competitors objectively you can self-analyze your own business.

This self-analysis helps you to answer the questions "What can I do better" and "how does my business or product rank compared to others". Personally, I like to reflect on the first question more than the second. Don't get hung up too much on what the competition is doing. You should be aware, but don't let it over influence you. Understand what you can do better, then do it.

COGS

One of the most important things that you can do for your business is to continually examine your Cost Of Goods Sold (COGS). The two biggest factors influencing the cost of nearly all products are the cost of raw materials and the labor involved to produce a finished part. Once you have a bit of history in your business producing a product or range of products you should have the information needed to reduce your costs.

I cannot tell you how many times I have heard "How can they sell that for so little!? I can't even buy my materials for that!". The two things that control the price of your materials are volume and source. By source I mean distance (the number of people, not miles) from the manufacturer.

Most makers start by purchasing materials that are easiest to obtain. This generally involves purchasing at retail outlets like Home Depot, Michaels, Hobby Lobby, the list goes on. If you are purchasing materials at a retail outlet, and purchase more than the typical retail customer does, then you are probably paying more for your raw materials than you need to.

While I still make occasional purchases at stores like these, most of the time it is because I want to make something with a material that I have never used before and just need one or two pieces. Once I begin making something for sale and plan to sell more than a couple, I find the best wholesale outlet possible. There may be a few levels to this as your volume expands and your cash flow improves.

As an example, I worked with a person who had some great graphic designs that would work well with night lights. They purchase 4 acrylic rounds with led light bases on a sale from a retail outfit. The original retail price with $19.99 and with 40% off and a coupon, they came out to $8.67 each after sales taxes. They made the first 4 prototype designs which worked well, and they sold immediately to the small test group that they showed them to.

With a bit of research, they found an identical product from an Amazon seller for $6.90 each if they purchased 25. For the next 100-150 units they sold, they order these. While the price allowed them to make a reasonable profit, they continued to do their research. Ordering a quantity of 200 or more from a seller on Ali-Express, they have since been able to get their price point below $5 a unit.

When ordering in this way however, delivery takes 45-60 days, so they need to plan appropriately and manage their inventory. Their average order is over $2500 now, so they carry significant inventory. And this is only one item. When you multiply this by the number of items you wish to offer, inventory carrying costs can be enormous. Getting the best per unit price may involve other sacrifices.

One other note on this particular item. One of the things that helped us find a source for it was the UPC code. While many companies produce their own version of a commodity product, in this case the products from the retail store were identical to those from Amazon. Including the UPC code. The UPC code identifies the manufacturer, which allows you to find them. While they are unlikely going to deal with you directly, they may direct you to one or more of their major sales outlets.

Another thing to consider when analyzing your COGS is material. Not "how inexpensively can I get this material", we've just covered that. This time I mean "Why am I making this product out of this material?". Having spent the past two years in supply chain Hell, I have worked with dozens of clients who cannot get the materials that they require. This has caused them to look for alternative options to these materials.

You would be surprised how often the answer to "Why do we use this material?" is "Because we always have." or "Because everyone does." Another common answer is "Because we have the machine and or tooling to make it from that." When your current material is no longer an option, you must innovate.

I recommend that you look at options as a part of your regular improvement process. Sometimes a product that you make from wood will be more durable in a plastic. Maybe that expensive coating material you are using isn't really needed. Maybe it is crucial for outdoor use in rainy weather, and you should offer a standard and "premium" version. There are a host of reasons for making material substitutions. Anytime that you can reduce cost and improve quality, go for it. Reduced quality at a lower cost? ... examine your product line and determine what you want to be known for.

Efficiency

The biggest cost in many products is the cost of labor. As your volume grows both the need and the ability to reduce your cost of labor rise. Starting with your highest volume products, you need to analyze the following parts of your production process, *Linearity, Commonality, Process*.

Linearity is the flow of a product through the creation process. When a maker starts out by making a single unit, the process is a completely linear one. The steps to complete the item are carried out in order, A-B-C-D. When making more than one it is most likely that carrying out these steps in series (as batches) will take less time per part making the process more efficient. For example, making 3 parts by doing AAA-BBB-CCC-DDD. While this is a simple and logical first step to increasing your throughput, many makers feel more comfortable with the A-B-C-D method and never progress.

I recommend that you run a series of tests on two small batches and see which method works best. It is likely that your efficiency running in series will be better. The larger the batch size, the more you can tune your processes over time.

Myself and many of the makers that I work with tend to have many products that have some level of common components. This can allow you to integrate the processes from several products together increasing the number of times you repeat a specific process.

Let's say, for example, we have two products to make, and we want 20 of each. The processes for product one is A-B-C-D. The processes for product two are B-E-F-G. Since each product requires that we perform process "B", maybe painting a piece white, we can do 20xA then 40xB (paint 20 parts white for product 1, then 20 more for product B) then finish up the C,D,E,F,Gs.

The more time that you spend in a single session repeating one step, for example painting pieces white, the more time you will think about it. When you think about a process over and repeatedly, you tend to examine ways to improve it. In our "paint it white" example, we might be thinking about how we can arrange pieces on a single surface to paint more without moving them. Maybe some simple holding fixtures would make this faster or easier. Maybe we stop using expensive, slow spray cans and get a small compressor and spray guns. Maybe ... you get the idea.

I spend a fair amount of time and money-making jigs, fixtures and purchasing specialty tools to make tasks not only faster, but easier. That last part is important. People aren't machines. The more "efficient" you make their tasks, the more repetitive they can be. If you can fully replace a task with a machine operation, great. If not, make sure that while you are making the process faster, that you are not making it more difficult. Making things more efficient can free up your and your employees time to focus on more important things.

25. REMNANTS

When you start a project with a brand-new sheet of material, whether it is a 10"x12" piece of vinyl or a 4'x8' sheet of steel, it is a rare occasion that you use the complete sheet. Getting every penny out of your materials is an important step in becoming successful in your business so managing these cut-offs, or remnants, can be an important step to increasing your profitability.

My personal approach to managing remnants has come from years of personal experience and frustration as well as the best practices from hundreds of manufacturers that I have had the good fortune to work with over my career. The approach varies greatly depending on the type and cost of material, the likelihood that remnants will get used, and the practical availability of well managed storage. I will break things down for you by material below.

Paper, Cardstock, Vinyl, and other small thin materials

When considering the use of these materials and the remnants that they create, we first need to discuss stock size. I have a good friend that has a vinyl poster business. She focuses almost exclusively on large format banners, signage, wraps and flags. She rarely works on anything less that 30" in length and cuts all of her vinyl on a 60" wide format cutter/plotter. In her business, she will trim off 10" wide strips, 6"x8" block and blobs of product all day.

The business will also have end cut remnants from these rolls that

145

are 24"-60" wide and a foot or so long. These remnants have little or no value to her as the setup time to cut a single piece of a large project on a roll feed cutter and piece it together later, outweighs the value of the vinyl. When considering remnant material, always remember that time is your most valuable resource and your remnant, sad as it may be, is worth less than your time to save it.

For those of you who are crying real tears right now thinking about the waste of materials, fear not. The business saves the majority of their "large scrap" and gives it to a local maker who does home décor and most of these prices find their way onto small hanging signs, car decals and a host of other items. I know a few large vinyl shops that donate their remnants to local makers and schools or sell their cutoffs at a steep discount. Some still find it too inconvenient to save and store their remnants and the sadly end up as trash.

As sales of small format vinyl cutters outnumber the sales of large format cutters by nearly 100 to 1, it is likely that more people here are concerned with what to do with small remnants that are created as they make their projects. Having spoken to dozens of people about how they manage their small remnants there are a few common themes and then there is the way that I do it. In my opinion the goal in keeping remnants is always to make sure that you are storing something of value that is worth more than your time to store and manage it.

One of the more common methods of keeping remnants whether they be paper, vinyl, leather or other thin products is to trim the remnant from your project and do your best to square those remnants up into somewhat usable shapes and sizes. Next you will sort by shape, size, and color and place them into clear plastic baggies or folder dividers (also clear) so that you can easily see what you have. One of the biggest failures tends to be storing small pieces of any type of material in a container that you cannot quickly see and locate the items.

Mixing items too much by size or mixing different colors or materials is an absolute recipe for disaster. In your mind you will be thinking "I have a piece of material of the right color in the right size for that somewhere" and spend the next 20 minutes searching for a $.15 piece of material.

My personal method for optimizing my remnants is a little bit different. I know from experience that I have different projects that I will repeat from time to time or season to season. When I create a new design and layout the project, I look for the areas surrounding the main project that would leave reasonably sized remnants. I then select from a large library of small bits and pieces that I reuse repeatedly throughout the year.

A few examples of this would be when I cut red or pink materials, I will surround the main project elements with a series of small hearts of standard sizes that I use in other projects throughout the year. When I cut black vinyl, I create a series of puppy paws around the outside of my project. White vinyl is usually used to create bunny ears for several Easter projects. Projects using primary colors lend themselves well to being surrounded by a series of letters that I use in two other projects. The majority of the time when I start cutting a new project, I cut either a full sheet or a half sheet. I have no 2x2 squares lying in wait.

These bunny ears, letters, and hearts along with numerous other items are cut to size and dropped into envelopes where I keep a quick tally of how many are available in my inventory. When Valentine's Day approaches, I know quickly that I have 375 hearts available that can be quickly added as surrounding decoration to other primary images. This saves a crazy amount of time during the busier times of the year.

3D printer materials

To be honest I have very little remnant material when working with my 3-D printers. Sure, I have my fair share of failed prints and some amount of spaghetti, but in terms of real remnant I have almost none. By far the largest amount of waste material is it in the form of black spools. While I have tried to find material that ships on cardboard spools, many brands that I use specifically still ship on plastic spools.

I have found a filament producer that will reuse the spools, but the shipping cost is higher than any cost reduction offered. While we do save and separate all the failed prints and waste, the volume has not yet reached a point that it is economical to have this material re-ground and extruded. At some point in the future our collected volume may make this worthwhile. Until then it continues to harmlessly accumulate.

One potential that I have seen a few very high-volume shops use is to purchase custom ordered "heavy spools" of material that come on oversized 10 kg reels and can be quickly rewound onto smaller spools. The primary costs savings here come from the high volumes purchased rather than any type of material saving.

Laser material - Wood, Acrylic and Leather
Once again when creating projects for the laser, I employ the technique of utilizing a full sheet for each run. This tends to be a little bit more complex than it is for paper or vinyl products as many of the materials that we use with our lasers come in a variety of sizes. When working with a custom project we start the initial layout on the smallest sheet that the project will fit on and attempt to surround or insert as many common objects as we can onto the sheet.

You might be curious at this point as to what types of common objects to create for materials like wood? Standard sized rounds can be used as wheels or decorations, standard sized gears can be used for various mechanical projects, slotted arch shapes are used as stands for a variety of items and Christmas items like snowflakes, sleds, candy canes, sleighs and ornaments get cut all year round.

Standard projects, ones which we create in batches, are often created across a series of sheets with parts for a single end product spanning multiple sheets. Depending on the size and shape of the parts and the nesting results, we often find that the larger the quantity of overall products, the more efficient the nesting of parts can be. For example, a toy with total of 13 various sized parts requires two 12x19 sheets and leaves a sizeable remnant.

That same toy however can be cut from a single 14x16 sheet with room for common parts and 3 can be run from a single 24x18 sheet with very little waste. At this point many of you who own the popular Glowforge will note that the 14x16 sheet will be a bit problematic and the 24x18 sheet will need to be cut in half.

The limitations of our machines will often drive our choices. In this specific case, a 12x19 sheet size limitation can be optimized by rearranging the parts to 16 of this toy on 23 sheets. This leaves the minimum amount of remnant material to be used for other small objects. Minimizing your remnant material will often require finding the optimum number of part combinations and does take time.

If you don't produce many common parts, or want to avoid the buildup of inventory, there is of course, another way.

On occasion I work with some materials that are very expensive. When using these products, I rarely want to produce any common items and wish to maximize the use of the material. In this case when I create the design, I include the overall profile of the original stock in my model. When I have completed the design, I save both the machine code to cut and engrave the parts as well as an outline file for the remnant. I label the remnant file with a simple alpha numeric code and save it. I label the physical remnant with the same code, usually on a wire twist tag and store it in a rack.

The next time I need to use the same material I will create just the design outline and see if it will graphically fit on any of my stored remnant files for the needed material. If so, I will repeat the process as before, this time storing the remnant file under the same name, but with an additional outline or set of outlines for the newly cut piece(s).

CNC Router remnants

Once again I must confess that I don't deal with much remnant material when working on CNC projects. In general, I cut stock to fit the project, machine the end product and any remnants are generally small and go to the waste bin. Some projects will leave areas that I can reuse, such as 2x2 blocks for one repeat product, but generally the remnants are odd shaped or too small to use for other projects.

Fear not, nothing goes to waste. Sawdust can go to the local farm and most of the remains are cut into small chunks perfect for a wood stove or fireplace. If you generate more than you need, check with the local boy or Girl Scout troops, they have never failed to take anything extra. Small pieces of more expensive woods tend to go to some wood carver friends.

However you decide to manage your remnants, regardless of the machine or process, always look for some way that the material can be used either for other projects or by someone else.

26. INVENTORY MANAGEMENT

Inventory. That one single word tends to spark emotion in nearly every long-term business owner that I know. Many lament the cost of carrying inventory as it ties up cash that they would rather put to other uses. (Usually, kids schooling or family vacations.) Others view their inventory as a strategic asset that allows them to compete with larger companies as it gives them the ability to deliver more quickly. Others still don't think much about their inventory, or don't have any. I think that this is a mistake.

You have probably heard the adage, "time is money". In business and to some degree in life, this is completely true. As an employee we directly trade time for money. I like to think about inventory in this same way in that inventory is "leveraged" money. Inventory is generally created with the combination of time and money and represent another store of value.

The value of the inventory can be viewed in two different ways. It can be view by its cost basis, the combined cost of the materials that went into creating it plus the time value of the effort that went into creating it or it can be viewed by its value basis, the price at which the product would sell. In this way inventory provides leverage, additional value, by storing the cost of materials plus the cost of labor until we decide to sell it, ideally returning all these costs, plus profit.

The upside of inventory is quite simple. Inventory allows you to minimize lost time by using time that would otherwise be idle or unused to create products that are yet to be sold. In its simplest example, you could work 364 days of the year creating products, all of which are sold on the 365th day of the year. Every 4th year you get one day off just for good measure.

In this simplest example, the only limit to the number of products that you could sell is the number of products that you could produce every day. If a day was missed for any reason, it could not be recovered. 363 days of products would be sold on the last day. Taking off weekends and a few holidays reduces typical output to 240 days' worth per year.

I am all for having ample time off. People need weekends to spend with friends and family and to recover from hectic weeks. Extended holidays help us to recharge and refocus, giving life meaning. That said, all workdays are not created equally.

Most businesses have wide fluctuations in the amount of product that they sell in each day, week, or month. The same therefore tends to go for product that is produced during that day, week, or month. The problem is that once a moment has gone, it cannot be recovered. Hoping that a financially good August will make up for a poor July can only happen if we can recover that time lost in July. That is achieved by building inventory.

Most maker businesses will work with three different types of inventories. Raw inventory are the materials that you purchase as inputs to your business. This is the flour and sugar at a bakery, the vinyl, plastic, or sheet goods of a maker. Semi-finished inventory are the materials that you have begun to process. The amount of processing may vary from simply cutting large sheets to standard usable sizes, to completing a sellable product except for some customization, like adding a name. Finished goods are exactly that, products that are ready to go to the end user customer.

The amount of investment varies across these types of inventories as does the flexibility as to what they can become in the end. The more work that is applied to the inventory, the closer it is to being sellable. There is however more risk of loss on finished goods if customer sentiment changes and people are no longer purchasing a certain product than there is on raw materials. As these raw materials are not yet turned into any specific product, changes in customer desire has less impact.

I like to look at Inventory in two ways. First it is a way for me to invest in my business when a strategic opportunity arises. This occurs when I add money into my company by purchasing inventory for the business. Usually this is when I purchase in large quantities to get better per unit discounts, or when I find specific items that I use frequently on sale.

Second, inventory provides me a way to continue to work on products when I have time more than the current orders that I have to fulfill. In both cases I am making an investment in my company by putting time and or money into the business.

There is a downside to building up excess inventory. That is the way that inventory is carried in your company books. Inventory is treated as an investment until the products created by that inventory are sold. That is, the money spent on inventory doesn't get deducted from company profits until that end products are sold, thus recapturing any profit or loss on this inventory. There are of course exceptions to this rule, so having an accountant and tracking your inventory purchases and draw down is important when calculating your profit/loss and taxes at the end of each quarter and year.

If you have sufficient cash flow to continue to invest in your business, and you can maintain that ability to roll excess inventory over from year to year, inventory can give you strategic advantages. Having the ability to meet the demands of your busiest seasons without overload, minimizing downtime for yourself and your employees, and being able to deliver volume requests in a more responsive manner will all make your business stronger.

Getting "too far over your skis" with inventory is always a risk. Creating excess inventory of products that fail to sell. Improper storage of inventory causing unusable goods. Improper tracking of your inventory causing missed deadlines or delays. These can all lead to losses that can rapidly eat into company profits, or core investment. Worse yet is being broke but having a fortune in inventory designed for sales tied to an event 3 months in the future.

If you plan your year well, manage your cash flow, grow your inventory gradually and strategically, and take advantage of special pricing opportunities, you will find that having well managed inventory will serve you well.

K is for Kite

While I was in grade school my father worked in a body shop and spent a lot of his time painting cars. One key ingredient in painting cars is masking them off which is done with giant rolls of a very thin paper. For a young kid on summer vacation there was nothing better than having a bundle of dowels and a giant roll of body shop paper. Throw in several rolls of grandmas thread for making doilies, I had the makings of a great summer.

The previous Christmas I had received a book on kites. It was amazing. It showed at least a dozen different types of kites. Diamond shaped kites, box kites, Japanese fighting kites and Chinese kites that were shaped like dragons. Every one of them had measurements and instructions. I was determined to make one of each by the end of the summer. I ended up with dozens.

My friends and I learned a lot about the dynamics of flying kites that summer. How tail length affects the kite, what shape was better, how to control a box kite and even how to get one of those giant Chinese Dragons up in the air. Spoiler alert, if you *can* get it up in the air, it will probably end badly.

As a kid, a kite is probably the perfect "make". Purchasing a kite was unheard of at the time and even if it was, it wasn't something you spent money on. It is the perfect platform to build, crash, repair, redesign, and repeat to see the different results. I think it's a bit sad that today's children are introduced to flying kites with a standard V shape flying wing constructed in plastic. There's no make left to it, you simply snap in a few pieces and go.

Most kids will never know the joy that I had of going downtown grocery shopping with my mother and seeing my kites miles away in the powerlines and trees of the city center. ☺

27. SALES OPTIMIZATION

Just like optimizing your maker processes can increase your daily output, optimizing your sales processes can maximize your sales. Sales optimization is a game of numbers and sometimes seemingly minor changes to a sales offering can have a dramatic impact on your sales. To optimize your sales, you will want to measure, and control, as many factors as you can. Sometimes details that you initially think they may not be important contain key insights. One thing is certain, you can't fix what you don't measure.

Presentation
Growing up, my parents were antique dealers. We traveled most weekends to shows across the country and setup shop in fields, tents, and buildings of every type. Depending on the location, we would pack a variety of tables, racks, stands, tablecloths, lighting, and all sorts of display accessories. Over the years my mother honed her display skills and had a reason for every choice that she made. Repeat that. She had a reason for every choice that she made.

White table clothes were for indoor use only, use them outdoors and they would look dirty by noon the first day. In the sun they were too bright. Blue showed clear glassware better, red was great at the holidays. Which products to cluster together and how far to space them were tested again and again. The most desirable item was placed at eye level, related items close by. All these details contributed to getting people out of the aisle and into our booth.

When setting up your shop, whether it is a retail establishment, a pop-up shop, a weekend event or an online store, the same type of rules apply. If you have a physical location or event, stand outside your booth while someone else is working it for you. Watch the people as they walk by. See what they notice first and what brings them into your booth. Change things from time to time and see what difference it makes. Walk past your shop from each direction, and most importantly, think like a customer.

While selling online makes it easier to reach more customers, it can make it harder for those customers to understand your product. Colors don't always look true in pictures, so I recommend providing plenty of images of your product against two or more background colors. Help the customer understand the size of your items by having items of known relative scale in the images with them.

Small items like jewelry should always be shown both on and off a model. Functional items should include a video. Items that require installation should have a guide available for the user to review at the point of purchase. Everything that you can do to improve the visual description of your item online will improve both your sales and your customer satisfaction.

I get on an airplane at least a couple of times a month. I have done this for years. Every time I hear the preflight announcements welcoming any first-time flyers I smile. Just because I do this all the time doesn't mean that everyone here does. The same is true for your products. Whether you recognized it or not, you are so close to your products that you take them for granted. Thinks like a first-time flyer when you list your product. Tell them everything. Assume they have never seen anything like it in their lives. Some of them may not have!

Search Engine Optimization

While your physical presentation is critical in a live setting and your images play an important part in your online presence, Search Engines still run on text. Search engines are the machines behind the machine, they are the ones who decide what websites to show you when you type something into the search bar on just about any homepage in the world. There is only one single secret that you need to know about search engines. Just one. They *want* to do a good job.

The single most important thing for a search engine is to do a good job. When you do a search, they want to return a set of results to you that contains a link to a page that satisfies your need for that search. Each of the search engine companies compete for business from advertisers, websites that use them as a plugin, and end users who rely upon them. If the results they return stink, people will opt for a different search engine. They don't want that; they want to do a good job.

To understand how they do that is straight forward. Every time a website page is created or changed a service for each search engine will find this updated page and scan it. By reading the text from your page they get a basic understanding of what your page is about. If you use the term "French Fries" 15 times on the page, chances are that the page is about "French Fries". Maybe the page also contains the term "Recipe". At this point, we pretty much know that the page is a recipe for French Fries.

The higher the frequency of the term "French Fries" as well as terms that the search engine recognizes as related to "French Fries", the more the search engine will trust you as a source for French Fry knowledge. "French Fry" in the title? Bonus points. Bold text? Bonus points. Italics? Bonus points. Spell and grammar checking? Bonus points. Search engines have learned to think like people.

The things that we like, they like too. The things that we place importance on, like titles and sub-titles, they do too. That is why larger fonts, and bold text get rated as more important. Think about that when you write your titles and descriptions for your items.

Because there are 26 million pages of French Fry recipes, these web crawlers dive even deeper into your page. If your page has multiple images on it this is a bonus, search engines know that people like images. If those images have what is known as alt-text, a text description of the image, it may raise the importance of this page if it deems the images add relevance. Something like "Step 1", "Step 2" as alt-text on images of a recipe page can increase the pages relevance to the search engine. Some more advanced search engines are starting to use the artificial intelligence that we have all been training for years "Pick all images containing flowers" to examine the images directly.

During the early days of the internet, bandwidth was limited, and search engine web crawlers ran less frequently and less deeply. This required that the page creator add a set of keywords and tags. The early crawlers only had to read the header of each page, containing these to be able to classify the page. They are still used today to allow the page creator to emphasize what words on the page are most important. Some search engines look at keywords, some look at tags and some consider both. They all have different weighting systems for them, so it is important to understand both.

Keywords

Keywords are exactly that. The words on your page that are key to the context of the page. Some publishing systems will pre-read your text before publishing it and determine the most used words, their location within sentences, and emphasis applied (bold, italics) and create a list of 10 words that are "key" to your page or article. These keywords are them loaded into the header section to help search engines better understand your page.

Some platforms allow you to manually override these, some don't. Many don't allow you to see or set them at all, those usually allow tag definition instead (which is different). Even if you don't see or have access to your keywords, keep in mind that whether your page creator generates keywords or not, search engines do. Word frequency, placement, and emphasis all impact what the search engine determines is most important to your page.

Tags

Unlike keywords, tags do not necessarily appear on your page. Instead, they are "hints" to help the search engines put your page into the appropriate categories for search. Tags do not appear on the page itself; they usually only appear in the header of the page which is hidden from the user. Many page creators allow you to manually input a series of tags (usually 10) which YOU feel are relevant to the pages content. When used correctly, tags can help improve the relevance of your page to the search engine and increase the search engines preference to return your page over someone else's.

Tags can present a bit of a double-edged sword, however. Since the search engine knows that these tags are manually entered by the user it takes a "trust but verify" position on your page initially. Let's say the search engine depends on your tag "French Fries" to display your page more frequently, but your page contains a bologna sandwich recipe. YOU think that people who are interested in French Fries would likely be interested in Bologna sandwiches as well. You can set your tags to be whatever you want, even irrelevant nonsense.

If your page is well received, that is users don't bounce to another page right away, you are ok. If, however, searches for French Fries that are directed to your page have a high bounce rate, that tag is marked as suspect for this page by the search engine. Too many suspects on a page and the page ranking (how often it will be presented as a search result) falls. Too many suspect pages within your site or sub site and the ranking of the whole site or sub site may be penalized.

User Testing

Understanding user preference when you are selling your items can mean the difference between moderate success and a windfall. But how do we know what customers want? We find out by testing them. By presenting them with the simplest choice, option 1 or option 2 and having them pick one. This is known as an A-B test and is the simplest way to find out what customers want. When offered two choices, do more people pick #1 or #2.

I look for opportunities to run A-B tests on consumers every chance that I get. At a live event you can show two different colors of the same product. Sometimes you will sell a near equal number of each, other times you will sell none of one version until the other sells out. With online advertising you can do some very advanced forms of A-B testing and when each ad campaign costs you money, getting 34 sales instead of 32 sales means a lot!

At one point in time, I did a fair amount of testing through user test sites. By using a user test site, you can poll people's reaction to your products prior to making them. By using high quality graphic mock-ups of potential products, you can understand how well it should sell before spending the money to make even one. This is best used when developing complex products that may require mold or other hard tooling that requires a great deal of up-front cost.

User testing sites can also provide feedback on a product, service or even a website design beyond just A-B testing, they could help you design tests that follow a multiple A-B-C path such as "If you liked A best, then which color" and "if you liked A in red, which size?" If you want to do usability testing, get feedback on website flow, or any other more complicated test type, investigate the options available through some of the user testing platforms that are available. Most of these sites can find an audience for you that can provide detailed written feedback on a product, image, website, etc. I have however found that these more robust user testing platforms have gotten expensive, and I find myself using them only during the prototyping stage.

Advertising

I have run a fair amount of online advertising over the past twenty years and one thing has always been true. I almost never run a single ad. Many years ago, when Netflix was just beginning, they ran sign-up ads all day every day. One day, after seeing the "same old" Netflix ad about seven times, the "Sign-Up Now" button moved from the left panel to the right. Curious I thought. Later that week it was back on the right, but the color of the button changed. Very interesting. Netflix, while probably not the first, was a pioneer in both internet advertising and user testing. At the same time.

Every ad that was run had two specific version. One with the button on the left, one with the button on the right. After 100,000 or so impressions (displays of the ad to a person), the ad with the button on the right had 3% more click through than the one with the button on the left. No other changes were made on the page. 200,000 people had spoken, and they wanted their button on the right. From that day forward the button was on the right. While 3% may not seem like much, it produces a significant savings in advertising costs.

If you are paying directly for views, the 3% savings can be seen directly. You pay a fixed amount for 100,000 views and instead of getting 124 customers, you get 128. Surprisingly though, even if you are paying for click-throughs, say "up to $1.50 per action", you will often find that "good" ads get charged slightly less than "bad" ads. Rather than paying an average of $1.37 per click you may get charged only $1.28 per click. What you say!? Yep. Remember how we discuss that search engines want to do a good job and they reward pages with low bounce rates and penalize those with high ones? The same is true for advertising engines. They don't want you to waste their views. If your ads require fewer views to get results, and pay the ad engine, they will run more and with better placement than others. Crappy ads? They may get click through, but the conversion rate on the clicks is likely to be less. In other words, the ad engine will give your crappy ad, crappy traffic.

Following this "always be testing" method of advertising, if you decide to run an ad, create two slightly different versions of it. One with a bolder font than the other or one with a dark blue background one with a pastel blue background. Rather than spending $100 a month on a single ad, spend $50 a month on each. You might think that text fonts don't matter that much, colors don't matter that much, what matters is my product and my ad being compelling! Yes, your product and ad need to be compelling, that should go without saying. One of your two ads however, will convert better than the other. When the difference is substantial, why would you want to continue to run the lower performing ad?

Demographics

Most online advertiser allow you to target your ads based upon some level of demographic, the statistical data defining the people that you advertise to. The simplest forms of demographics are gender, location, and age. More advance demographics might identify interests, marital status, income, and others. When advertising you need to use these to your advantage whenever possible.

If your product is designed for women with young children, you should immediately narrow your age range to above 16 and below 40. While these are not absolute boundaries, they cover your "sweet spot" in age. If your advertiser has information on children, then filter down to limit to only those with children. These demographics allow you to do some logical narrowing of your advertising which reduces the number of poorly targeted ad displays. I might run 2 ads side by side initially. One that is women with children only and one with all women of the desired age.

Chances are good that women with children have girlfriends their age that may not have children yet. They may purchase your product as a gift whereas the ones with children may purchase for themselves. Run both and see which converts best.

Should we run a third one with men only? Yes, probably. We could possibly run other groups as well targeting potential grandparents or other groups. There is however a catch. When ad engines get a new ad, say "spend up to $50 this month", they try to front load them a bit. In other words that may try to get four or five days of results in the first 24 hours. This helps them figure out where to run your ad, how well it works and how much priority it should get. When you start your ads, give it 8 hours or so and then check the results. The last thing that you want to do is to spend your whole ad budget to display 3 million views to consumers in Asia while you sleep. Not that I don't love Asia, personally some of my favorite places are there, but I don't ship to them.

Oh, yeah. I've done that. Remember that demographics should allow you to narrow by geography. Always filter out countries that you don't ship to. You may also want to filter out non-native language sites. Not always, as English is the first or second language in a wide variety of countries, but most times I will limit to English speaking countries. I may run a separate ad (or set of ads) in EU countries where English is widely understood. If you do ship to other countries and can support customers in their language, you may want to add ads in their native language.

By combining your demographic data with A-B testing you can find continual ways to tweak your ads to improve your overall conversion ratio and seek out more customers. Most of my initial ads have at least four versions. Once I narrow my range of customers by geography, age, language, and country I will create a base ad to run. I will then split by gender to see whether the ad performs better to men or women. I will then split each of these to run 2 different version of the base ad, usually changing either the color of the ad or the main image of the ad. A short run of these 4 combinations may show some surprising variations in preference.

As enough data comes in for each ad pair to make a comparison, replace the poor performer with another hopeful option. Repeat, repeat, repeat. You may or may not be surprised to find that you end up running strikingly different ads for different segments of your customer base to get the best results.

Own your Audience

I get asked a lot about my preferred advertising platforms. The answer is simple, the ones that I own. Not that I own Facebook, Google, Amazon, or any of the other platforms, what I own is the location of the ads first contact. "What the heck do you mean" you ask? Let me explain.

A huge percentage of makers start out with a shop on Etsy. A huge percentage of Etsy shop owners also get frustrated with the fees and terms on Etsy. Over time many will migrate to other platforms or their own websites so that have better control over their sales. Herein lies the problem. If you begin advertising and spending money directly with Etsy to have them advertise on your behalf, all of the traffic goes directly to their store. When running "Etsy Ads", this really is the only options that you have. You also have limited control over the insights gained from the traffic that you are generating. Etsy know the demographics of the customers who click through those ads to your shop, but you have little insight.

If you are directly running ads on other platforms, such as Facebook, Google, etc, you have control over both the demographics you use for your ads as well as exactly what you are advertising. You could, from these other ad platforms, advertise your products and send the viewer directly to your Etsy shop. You could also, direct them somewhere else. Where you ask? How about YOUR business Facebook page or YOUR Instagram, or YOUR website directly.

By directing your Ad traffic to your Facebook page, you can then present a post or video showing one of your products or how it is made. Same with Instagram, your own site, or any other platform site where you have ownership of the content and the user ID. Once viewing your post, image, or page, you can provide the link to your Etsy shop. If you provide a tracking link, you gain insight into which of your posts produce the best click through rates. Since you own this content, if you ever elect to move from Etsy to another platform, in some cases you can modify your content to point to the new location.

Even if the user decides not to click through to your sales page, you may gain a follower on one of your social platforms. Best case? You get both!

R is for Radio

One summer, while at a flea market, I came across the seller who had a large box of radio equipment that he was selling. He wanted a fair amount of money for it, more than I had at the time, and I was disappointed to walk away. However, If you have ever been to a flea market you know that there are two good times to make a purchase. The first time is in the early morning as people are setting out their goods. Sometimes they have no idea what they have and are selling it for a very low price. The next best time is at the end of the day as the seller is packing up. If the seller has had a very good day, they may be in the mood to give you a bargain. If the seller has had a bad day, they may need a little bit of money to get through the week. The end of the day was my striking point for the radio equipment.

As soon as I got home I went straight to work. I created a giant antenna from some aluminum tubing and my father helped me mount it to the roof of the garage. We tuned to the antenna so that would work properly and I got to work on the radio.

The radio that I had purchased used pairs of crystals and had a huge variety of frequencies available. I chose a couple of short wave and several on the citizen band that were popular at the time. While my initial results were pretty good the radio itself just didn't seem to have enough power. At the time a five-watt radio was the standard and could broadcast many miles but living in a rural community there just weren't many people to talk to.

For me, the solution was obvious. Amplification.

On a Wednesday morning that summer as I was talking to a truck driver going down the highway 60 or so miles from my home, I received a visit from my neighbor Jeff.

Jeff happened to live a few houses behind us and was several years older than me, but I knew him through his younger sister. Jeff also happened to be a member of the local police force. It seems that my radio was interfering with our local police and fire radio! Amplification came with unintended consequences.

Over that summer I learned how to tune crystals to stay very narrowly within their bands and how to build a better amplifier with much less noise. The result was not only keeping my power and distance without interference but also showing other people how to get better distance from their radios.

While I would like to say that this was the only visit that the police made to our home, it was not. Living in a small town made for a tight knit community. Both of my parents were on our local emergency squad and knew the entire force. After a while every time a car pulled into the driveway I didn't know whether it was for a social visit or if I had done something a little bit outside the realm of acceptable once again.

While I'm still not sure sometimes whether it is better to ask permission or forgiveness, I do know that sometimes pushing the boundaries results in breakthroughs of knowledge.

28 MANAGING YOUR MONEY

The very first thing that I recommend you do when starting your business is to open a separate checking account. Whether this is setup as a business account or a personal account is largely a matter of your banks policies and costs, but you need to separate your personal funds from your business funds right away. Beyond that, I recommend that you open a separate personal savings account as well. Why is that you ask? Most small businesses start as sole proprietorships and most small businesspeople run their own payroll for at least the first year or so.

Having these three separate accounts will allow you to treat your payroll and taxes in a professional manner from the start. Enforcing such discipline early on in your business may not be much fun, but it can save you from running into one of the most common troubles in small business. Trouble with the tax man. Until you have reached the point where you have engaged a payroll company to manage your tax withholdings, here is a basic approach to managing your business finances.

Establish your business checking account. You will be funding this yourself from your personal funds, or from funds borrowed from friends or family. If you are funding this yourself, consider it a sunk cost and move on. If you have borrowed to get started, you will need to manage this as a loan and the repayment of it will need to be tracked in your accounting software. If you are borrowing money from outside sources for your startup you should be consulting an accountant right from the start so that they can advise you how to best manage this for your business type.

ALL earnings go into this account, including cash collected at live events. All sales need to be tracked and listed in your accounting as earnings. All expenses for the business such as materials for your products, event costs, packaging, shipping, equipment, insurance, etc are all paid for directly from your business account. Yes, these can be paid for on a company credit card with the card being paid for from the business account, but I will caution you on using credit cards to fund your business. The cost is far too high.

If all is going well with your business, the account balance will begin to grow. Hopefully it will grow rapidly and at some point, you will want to begin taking distributions from the company. Once you have reached this point it is important to manage the flow of funds wisely. For our example we will assume that your business is doing very well, and you feel that you can safely distribute $2000 each month to yourself as a salary.

We will start by transferring, or writing a check, from your business account to the savings account. This saving account will serve as an intermediary between the company and you. The savings account will then distribute a portion of the business's distribution to you directly by transfer to your checking account. This will be your net pay. The remainder will be held in the savings account and accumulated until the next quarterly tax payments need to be made.

For our example we will assume that we expect to earn $24,000 from our business this year and that we have $25,000 in other income. This will place us in the 12% tax bracket for 2022, so we need to account for this. We will look at other examples in the chapter about taxes.

Using our $2000 distribution as an example, we will then transfer 70% of that ($1400) to our checking account and withhold 30% here for taxes. 30% for taxes! What! You just said 12%!

While the federal tax rate on this income will be 12%, you will also need to account for 12.4% for social security (6.2% as an individual and 6.2% as your employer) plus 2.9% for Medicare. Assuming a couple of percent for your state and local taxes and setting aside 30% seems about right. When we talk about higher numbers or working spouses in the chapter on taxes you will see that some people should be setting aside 40-50% or more and that failure to do so can quickly leave you in a very bad situation.

The alternative, one that I highly recommend as you establish your business, is to use a payroll company. The payroll company will operate as that middle savings account, receiving a check or electronic deposit from your business, remitting your taxes to all relevant governments, and sending you a check or electronic deposit into your personal account for the net proceeds.

This service is available as an add on to Quickbooks or from a wide variety of payroll services such as Paychex, Paycor, ADP and others. While it can seem expensive when first starting out, it greatly simplifies your efforts in tracking your personal taxes from business income.

If you are diligent and stick to a distribution plan such as this all will be well. If you are conservative, such as these numbers are, you are likely to have real saving available in this account at the end of the year when you reconcile your taxes. You will however need to avoid the traps that financial pressures put on us from time to time.

When it comes time to make a distribution but there is only $1000 available, what do you do? What you don't do is distribute it all directly to yourself so you can pay your bills. You send it to the saving account, and you distribute your normal percentage. Things get really tough; do you rob the savings account to pay your bills? Well, you know my answer and you know yours. I hope that you can avoid this, but we have all been there from time to time. Do your best to avoid big trouble by fixing little trouble.

While the most common issue with a startup business is having too little money, having more than you are used to can also be a problem. The first instinct is to distribute it to yourself as a bonus or increasing your personal payroll. I highly encourage you to resist this temptation for as long as is possible. The longer that you can run your business profitability, and the more personal sacrifice that you endure, the more cash flow that is available to fund your company and ensure that the cash keeps flowing.

If you find yourself with a profitable business that is producing excess cash flow you should always be looking for ways to make it even better. Is there capital equipment that the business would benefit from? Can you put an additional employee to work in a productive manner? Should you be building additional inventory for future events? Should you be investing in better physical displays, web presence or advertising? There are always productive ways to put excess capital to work.

Once your business is well established and can weather the majority of seen and unforeseen events, then you can begin to reap the rewards of building your business more aggressively. The biggest reason for small business failures is an unexpected decline in cash flow. As a founder, your job is to protect the business even when that means putting its survival ahead of your desires.

29 TAXES

One of the things that seems to come as a surprise to many of the first-year business owners that I talk with is taxes. As I discussed in the previous section on managing your money, preparing for your quarterly and year end taxes should be done as a part of your monthly expense management.

Sales Taxes

While payroll/income taxes will take the largest tax bite out of your revenue, they are not the only tax that you need to be aware of. State sales tax collection is required in more than 40 states in the U.S. Depending on the state, and the amount of tax collected, you will be required to remit a payment to the state treasury either yearly, quarterly, or monthly.

Businesses with high turnover, those collecting large amounts of sales tax, are required to settle their accounts at the end of the day. Businesses such as bars, restaurants and large retailers remit taxes through electronic transfer at the end of each day in many localities.

Your legal obligation is to collect sales taxes due in any state that you have a physical establishment in. You are required to collect them statewide, but at a varying rate depending on the location where the transaction took place. Let's look at a quick example.

For our example we will have our business located in Columbus,

Ohio, a state which requires you to collect sales taxes on all products and services sold within the state. The tax rates of the state of Ohio is currently 5.75%, with county and local taxes, the collection rate in Columbus is 7.5%. All business that you conduct at your location requires you to collect 7.5% in taxes and remit them to the state on a schedule based upon your total sales volume. Most of the time that will be quarterly.

How about if you decide to setup at an event in Cleveland, Ohio? The local taxes in the Cleveland area are slightly higher and, as a business registered with a location in Ohio, you are required to collect taxes at the point of sale. For this event, you will be collecting taxes at the 8% rate and identifying them as such with your filing.

Selling by mail to any customer in Ohio? Yep, you will need to collect taxes for the sale based upon the customers location as that is the point of transaction. Sound a bit complicated? It is. Thankfully there are several services that can be used for electronic transactions that automatically calculate the taxes for you based upon the shipping zip code of the customer.

If you are selling to a broad audience within your state, having a robust POS system to track your individual sales can be an essential tool to managing not only your sales, but simplifying your tax collection.

How about selling to a customer outside of your state? It used to be that if you did not have a physical presence in the state, you were not required to collect taxes on the sale. The end user customer was expected to calculate how much they have spent on products with out of state vendors and pay the required sales taxes as a "use tax" with their tax returns. As you can guess, this didn't happen, and you are now required to collect taxes for out of state sales above certain threshold levels set be each state.

Some states allow you to sell as much a certain amount of of product before they require you to collect. Others start with your first dollar of sales. With 45 states in the U.S. having a state sales tax and each having their own set of rules, it can get tricky. Having an automated system to track, collect and remit these payments is a necessity if you wish to distribute broadly.

This last bit is why nearly all the selling platforms that combine business to customer sales from a large group of sellers to a large group of buyers (think Etsy, EBay, Amazon, etc) have mechanisms in place to collect and remit taxes to all the states and localities requiring such online sale collections.

One of the benefits to selling through an online platform is this very thing. Collection and remittance of state and local taxes is managed automatically by the platform. This single benefit of selling via a platform is worth a significant portion of the (sometimes outsized) fees that they charge. The platform simply sends you your selling price minus fees, fees, and more fees, and you recognize that money as the net revenue collected for the product.

What if you sell a lot at events and a significant portion of the transactions are in cash? Handling all the coinage that is required for a large number of sales can be time consuming and frankly, a pain in the rump. Looking at our Columbus example, a $22 sale would result in the collection of $23.65. $22 for your product and $1.65 (22*0.075) for the state of Ohio and the localities around Columbus.

Your option in this case would be to charge $24, taxes included. To calculate the remittance to the state you would divide the total collected by 1.075. This would provide you with $22.3246 for your product and $1.6754 for state taxes. Yes, I carry this out to 4 digits for this example as I only round up at two digits (favoring the penny to the state) after combining all sales. Let's say 1000 units sold for $2400. That results in $2232.46 for you and $167.54 for the state.

I am not an accountant, and this should not be taken as financial advice other than to produce an awareness of what your obligations are regarding collecting sales taxes in your state. I recommend that all small businesses that sell direct to the public either use a POS system or work with an accountant to handle sales tax matters.

While you should certainly be able to manage the collection and remittance of these taxes on your own, this is one area that I recommend a second set of experienced eyes to review your work. The cost of doing so is likely to be less that the costs incurred if you get it badly wrong.

Income Taxes
When starting your business, it is likely that you will be a sole proprietor until there is a reason to change to another form of business operations. For our purposes here we will assume that is the case for our examples unless otherwise noted.

While the accounting changes with an LLC or Corporation, the general principals set forth when starting as a sole proprietor remain the same.

Throughout the business year you will need to calculate and pay a series of taxes using a variety of tax forms. If the thought of managing your own taxes seems overwhelming, or worse yet causes you to not act on them, you are not alone. Many first-time business owners, while able to take on the toughest problems in their chosen field, freeze with fear when it comes to doing their taxes. I fully understand as I used to postpone preparing taxes for fear of bad news. If this sounds like you, there are two choices. Education and assistance. I recommend both.

While I will repeat that I am not an accountant or financial advisor of any kinds, I have been involved in filing of taxes for sole proprietors, partnerships, llcs and corporations for several years.

Having the ability to prepare your own tax forms and understand your business before turning them to an accountant for review is an important and powerful skill when running your own business.

What I will do here is to give you a basic understanding of the timeline, processes and forms required to understand your own taxes as a sole proprietor. For simplicity we will assume that you have started your new business on the first of January and process your revenue on an ongoing basis.

As an employee of a company, you receive a salary, equally distributed throughout the year. When you join the company you complete a W-2 form which declares how many deductions you will take and whether you have a working spouse or other income. These pieces of information are used to determine how much of your salary goes directly to you and how much is withheld for taxes.

Being self-employed, or being a sole proprietor, you need to use this same information though you will be making some assumptions about your "salary", or in this case your net profit from the business. This information will help to determine how much we should be withholding for taxes when we make a distribution to ourselves.

Personal income taxes in the U.S. and many other countries work on a graduated scale. The more you make, the higher the percentage you will pay in taxes. Federal taxes on your first $10,000 of earning will be close to zero while taxes on the same amount on top of a large salary could be more than 50%. Given such a wide variance you can see why it may be important to plan accordingly.

To understand this better I have included the 2022 personal income tax rate table on the following page. Always be sure to reference the tables directly from your tax forms or software.

For 2022 the tax rates for personal income are as follows:

Tax Rate	For Single Filers	For Married Individuals Filing	For Heads of Households
10%	$0 - $10,275	$0 - $20,550	$0 - $14,650
12%	$10,275 - $41,775	$20,550 - $83,550	$14,650 - $55,900
22%	$41,775 - $89,075	$83,550-$178,150	$55,900 - $89,050
24%	$89,075 - $170,050	$178,150 - $340,100	$89,050 - $170,050
32%	$170,050 - $215,950	$340,100 - $431,900	$170,050 - $215,950
35%	$215,950 - $539,900	$431,900 - $647,850	$215,950 - $539,900
37%	$539,900 or more	$647,850 or more	$539,900 or more

As an example, we will compare how much we need to set aside from our $40,000 of expected business income under two different circumstances. First, we will examine our tax burden as a single person with no other income and secondly as one of a married couple with $100,000 in other combined income.

For our single person with no other income, taking a standard deduction of $12,950 you will be paying taxes on $27,050 ($40,000 - $12,950). For the first $10,275 we will pay $1,027.5 (10%) For the remaining $16775 we will pay $2013 (12%) for a total federal tax of $3041.50. But wait...there's more.

As this is earned income and you are both the wage earner and the employer, you are required to pay Social Security and Medicare taxes on all your income. This is calculated from the first dollar (without your standard deduction) and continues to $147,000. For our single taxpayer we will pay 12.4% (6.2% employer, 6.2% employee) for Social Security and 2.9% (again, equally split) for Medicare. This represents a total tax of 15.3% or $6,120.

When we combine Social Security, Medicare, and Federal Income taxes we see that we have a combined total a bit over $9,000. This is a bit higher than your actual payment will have to be as you do not pay taxes on the income taken by social security taxes and visa versa. The net total runs about 92% of this or $8200.

If you expect to withhold somewhere between these two numbers, you can be confident to not run into trouble.

Provided that your income comes in roughly even throughout the year, your quarterly federal tax withholding will be just over $2000 a quarter. If you see more, or less, income in a quarter than expected, adjust accordingly.

Our married couple will also take the standard deduction, this time of 25,900. That leaves our couples base income at $74,100. This will have us paying 12% on the $9400 that takes us up to $83,500 or $1128 (12% of $9400) plus 22% on the remaining $30,600, an additional $6732. Our total federal taxes on the $40,000 of additional income is $7860.

Again, we have the same Social Security and Medicare taxes of $6120 giving us a total of $13980. The same tax-on-tax reduction drops us to about $12,500 or $3125 a quarter. You can see from just these two examples, with the taxes varying from around $8k to $13k, that preparing accordingly is important to avoid a nasty surprise when reconciling at the end of the year. The same preparation needs to be considered when planning for your state and local taxation as well.

While these examples are simple and ignore a host of factors, it provides a primer on what you should be prepared for.

W is for Welder

When I was 14 years old, I purchased a 1965 Pontiac Lemans from my sister. The Lemans was the larger and less desirable brother to the Pontiac GTO. While the engine was the largest model available for the car, the body itself was much longer than the GTO and its weight distribution was all in the back end. Topping it all off was, of course, a top. Everyone knows that a convertible is the only way to go. Whether I had acquired an unrealistic amount of confidence in my thus far short life, or simply didn't know any better, I decided to turn what I had into what I wanted.

My plan was simple. Remove the roof, cut 14 inches out of the middle of the car, remove the back seat, and reduce the trunk by 22 inches. Most of the work didn't faze me in the least. I had cut, aligned, and brazed almost every panel of a car together by this time already. Replacing the floor and building a trunk lid door would both be a bit time consuming, but achievable. The one real problem would be cutting the frame.

Shortening the frame of the car to remove the back seat would require taking the same 14 inches out of the frame and floor as I would behind the driver's door. The problem here is that the gas welder we had just didn't produce heat fast enough to give a reliable weld on thick metal. Since I was removing the roof, I would also need to reinforce the frame to make sure that the body was stiff enough to not twist. The solution was professional welding equipment. That, was all I wanted for Christmas!

Getting a welder was not a small request. While my parents were always supportive of my projects, a welder was a big financial commitment for us. I did have one thing going for me though. My father operated welding equipment at work all the time.

Dad had experience working in a frame shop when he worked in the truck depot and deep down inside, I knew that he would really like to have one at the house. We made a deal. If I could complete all the other work required on the build, he would consider a welder for Christmas.

Remember that trench I talked about when we discussed electricity. Well, that trench delivered the 220 V that a new welder would require. Christmas delivered the welder!

It was still 40 degrees out the day that my father and I welded that frame together. The doors lined up. The wheelbase was almost perfect. The amount of work to be done now that the frame was complete was enormous!

Over the next 18 months that car was cut to pieces and reassembled to a running, driving convertible. Along the way several other small specialty tools were bought, dozens of new skills were learned, and a lot of potential pitfalls were avoided. This project above all others taught me that while you can achieve results by "making do", having the right tools makes everything easier. It also taught me that the first time you do almost anything, you don't know how much you don't know. Having experienced guidance is another lifesaver. Without my father to guide me that car would have ended up scrap a long time before it did.

The car did eventually end up moving on to somebody else. The project became too large for a high schoolers budget. In truth it always was, but I didn't know that when I started. The build itself however was worth every cent invested and every hour spent. Some might call it a failure; I call it the world's best education. Remember that the next time you find yourself in deep water trying to doggy paddle to the edge.

30. THE MAKERS CALENDAR

Everyone knows that the Christmas holiday season is responsible for greater than average sales in most stores, but just how big is this end of year swing? For most retailers, the last quarter of the year accounts for about 27% of their sales, so just a little more that you would expect if sales were the same across all four quarters. This of course is an average which includes a wide range of businesses.

While grocery sales are up due to holiday binge eating and gasoline and travel sales surge as more people travel to see family, the real "tale of the tape" is in the retail shopping numbers.

Toys and Home Décor as examples, sales from just the last two months of the year, November and December, often account for as much as 35% of all sales. Without this year end rush, many, if not most, retailers would not be able to survive the coming year. For small businesses, the numbers can be even more skewed towards holiday sales with many reporting that 50% or more of their income comes in November and December.

With so many Maker businesses focused on Home Décor, Apparel and gift items, it's no wonder that those Makers recognize much of their revenue during the holidays. Many of the Makers that I speak with around that time of year are almost frantic trying to fill orders and they themselves don't have the opportunity to enjoy the season. They need a better calendar.

We discussed early on that there is a lot to be learned from a Gardener when it comes to running a business. One of the most important things is time management. Every successful gardener knows that the planting of the garden starts months before a single seed goes in the ground. The same is true for every successful maker business. With a proper calendar you will breeze through the year-end holidays while eliminating any long periods of inactivity earlier in the year.

Creating your calendar starts with the major holidays that you will be making products for. Some creators will try to address every major yearly event while others will focus on the holidays that mean the most to themselves and their families. I have no problem with either approach however I focus on the holidays that fall in line with my upbringing and experiences. I find that having a connection to the products helps you to be a better maker.

We will begin our calendar with the major U.S. holidays. If you live in a different region you will want to start with those holidays that are biggest in your area. If I had to pick just a dozen to start with, I believe that the biggest opportunities would be something like this:

1. New Year's Eve/Day. Don't forget that the end of the traditional year is not the only end of year celebration to consider, Chinese New Year at the end of January is wildly popular as well.
2. Valentine's Day.
3. Saint Patrick's Day.
4. Easter.
5. Mother's Day.
6. Memorial Day.
7. Father's Day.
8. Independence Day.
9. Labor Day.
10. Halloween.
11. Thanksgiving.
12. Christmas.

The month of December is make or break for many retailers. Whether you personally celebrate Hanukkah, Christmas, Kwanzaa or one of the other religious or secular celebrations this month, many use this time of the year as a major gift giving celebration.

If those major American holidays aren't enough, there are dozens of other widely celebrated holidays that you may want to consider. A quick scan of my own calendar shows a few dates that I mark with some of my friends.

- Mardi Gras
- Groundhog Day
- Super Bowl
- Martin Luther King Day
- April Fool's Day
- Passover
- Ramadan
- Cinco de Mayo
- Juneteenth
- Diwali

In fact, the Jewish and Islamic calendars have numerous milestones scattered throughout the year. While many of these are more subdued events, several are celebrated with gift giving and a well-made, thoughtful product would be very welcome.

Having been blessed to get to know people from around the globe, I realize that my personal knowledge of others tradition is microscopic. If you partake in cultural celebrations that are outside of the widespread norms of the area that you live in, embrace those traditions, and use your talents as a creator to service these peers. Providing heartfelt products and services that celebrate underserved events can be rewarding in many ways.

How about those major events that you don't really have a personal connection to or know very much about? Well, rather than try the "fake it till you make it" strategy here, I recommend that you take a different tact. Find a partner. I have no personal connection to Juneteenth, Diwali, Cinco De Mayo, and a host of other celebrations. I have partnered with other small business to provide materials, products, and services to enable them to better meet the needs of their customers at times of the year when they are the busiest. Everyone wins.

Once you have filled your schedule with general events, the ones that everyone will be competing for, look for your personal events. Design products for Dogs or Dog Lovers? Pencil in the major Dog Shows or other properly themed events that you might want to prepare for. Does your local area provide any appropriate events? Search them out and add them to your schedule.

With the major time sensitive items laid out on your calendar you can then examine the types of life events that you might want to address. Do you make products that lend themselves well to Birthdays? Anniversaries? Weddings, Funerals, Divorces? If you focus on any of these milestones (other than Weddings, which are big in the summer) you may benefit from finding blocks of time to prepare products for these. Having inventory for birthdays available during other major holidays allows you to deliver without interrupting your focus on the holiday opportunity.

If you start laying out your calendar with the major holidays that you will be designing and creating products for, you will have a solid foundation of opportunity. If you create rough estimates of how much product you feel you will need to have to address each one you can then determine how much effort, and therefore time, will be required to meet these opportunities. This can drive your overall schedule, cash flow, and inventory needs.

Large companies have teams of people who pour over previous year's sales figures, examine competition and alternatives to their products, and assess product sales potential all in an effort to determine how much of each product needs to be produced when. Planning for special holiday editions of a product may begin a year or more in advance. As each of their products may have common materials, coordination across all their products may produce savings through increased buying power or may require adjustments due to limited supplies. The same planning, at a smaller scale, should be a part of your process.

If, for example, you estimate that Christmas will give you the opportunity to sell 500 of your best-selling product, you have a target. If you determine that each one will take twenty minutes to create and require $3 of materials, you know that you will have to find roughly 180 hours of labor and $1500 for that effort. If you are the sole person in the business, you will quickly realize that you need to start making at least 4 weeks prior in order to deliver on time.

Provided that you have adequate cash on hand, you could potentially create a significant portion of these, let's say 250-300 during the summer months when things are slower. This gives you a head start on a very busy time of year and limits your risk of slow year-end sales by not creating 100% of the inventory you expect to sell. This may also allow you to begin selling earlier in the season increasing your overall sales.

I know that for many people who are just starting out it can be very difficult to think about a holiday nine months in the future when you are busy trying to find a sale this week. As your business starts to grow however it can be extremely empowering to finish the products you need for this week, look up at your planning board, and know exactly what inventory you should be building for next week, next month or even the month after.

As you begin to plan each potential product offering for each potential opportunity you will, hopefully, begin to find yourself with a very full calendar indeed.

V is for Vanity Card

If you've made it through the end of the book with me I want to thank you. I hope that something within these pages helps you along your journey and allows you to turn what you love into what you do.

I also hope that these little inserts, vanity carts as I call them, help you to find some inspiration in your creation. You will notice that many of these come from my very early childhood. Making and creating has been in my blood since as early as I can remember.

If you take away one small thing from these silly little cards may it be this; share your drive to make things with someone very young. Teach them to embrace their curiosity and help them to become a maker at heart. Show them that pursuing an advanced degree, while admirable, may not be the only path to success. Help them to find things that they love because the more things that they love, the more options they have in the future. Above all share your knowledge and your excitement freely and openly, the future depends on you for it.

Oh, one last thing. I do know that V comes before W, but nobody is perfect 😊

ABOUT THE AUTHOR

I have always been making things. One of my earliest memories is of me in my closet, cutting and taping together some sort of machine. I can't remember the machine, but I do know that it had rubber bands and levers and when I finally completed it and pulled the lever ... zing! A brief second or two of some Rube Goldberg like motion and I was hooked. I must have been quite young because I was making it in my closet, untrusted to be left alone with scissors!

Fast forward fifty or so years and I am still hooked on making. My tools are now a bit more robust than scissors, but the concepts are the same. Design, cut, assemble, test. Whether it is paper, vinyl, and wood or plastic, steel, and aluminum, I still get excited at the prospect of something new.

Beyond just making, I really enjoy the feeling that you get when you help someone else improve their processes. Sharing my knowledge of business, machining, automation, and process improvement has become my favorite make. Making better makers, for me, is the ultimate and I hope that I can help you in some small way.

What started with a set of encyclopedias from my parents has evolved into a lifetime of experimentation. If my parents taught me one thing it is that education is not an event, it's a lifelong journey.